ANCHOR]

FLICKERINGS

First published in Great Britain in 1994 by
ANCHOR BOOKS
1-2 Wainman Road, Woodston,
Peterborough, PE2 7BU

Foreword

Anchor Books is a small press, established in 1992, with the aim of promoting readable poetry to as wide an audience as possible.

We hope to establish an outlet for writers of poetry who may have struggled to see their work in print.

Following our request in the National Press, we were overwhelmed by the response. The poems presented here have been selected from many entries. Editing proved to be a difficult and daunting task and as the Editor, the final selection was mine.

The poems chosen represent a cross-section of styles and content. They have been sent from all over the country, written by young and old alike, united in the passion for writing poetry.

I trust this selection will delight and please the authors and all those who enjoy reading poetry.

Michelle Abbott
Editor

CONTENTS

NATURAL REBELLION

Man's moods are the seasons
Man's soul is the sky
The earth is a cradle carved specially for thee
A child needs a mother
Nature needs a child
And she nurtures its branch on the evolutionary tree.

An intimate relationship
Life's whispered consent
An unrehearsed alliance 'tween the crude and the pure
Man born to nature
Lives in privileged pretence
Dipping fingers into knowledge with inquisitive innocence.

The quiet winds of intellect
Penetrate passive dreams
Forging visions of grandeur on impressionable minds
No code of behaviour
Just freedom en-masse
Thus an exodus stumbled from a primitive past.

A marriage of optimism
In a primordial love
Of some broken promises permeating the wild
Some words of disagreement
A liaison in doubt
'Tis a natural rebellion between mother and child.

A spiritual adolescence
Only a mother would know
The choreographed sequence of ignorance and guile
The moods are the seasons
The tantrum our voice
'Tis a natural rebellion from the mouth of a child.

David Bridgewater

MEMORIES

When slicing beans for dinner
my mind went back to Dad.
To the Dad of many years ago,
who then grew green and tender veg.

He always sliced the beans
for Sunday dinner.
After he had gathered up his crop.
He would sit on the back doorstep
in the summer.
Slicing carefully and slowly
with precision.
Every cut an offering from his plot.

He would often sing to help
along the rhythm
In his sweet and clear toned
tenor voice.
Ballads, old-fashioned now -
of long ago.
I'll Take You Home Again Kathleen
and *Alice Where Art Though?*

The silver birch he planted
when first wed
Stood watching his commitment
to the task.
Their dainty leaves sun-dappling
the pathway.
But all that was very long ago.

Joan Clark

FOR MY MOTHER ... xxx

The praise may go out to she who breathed life
Into my heart, body and unto my soul.
Who I burdened with my presence, my trouble and my strife
Who filled me with the spirit to achieve future goals.
Throughout suffering, searing pain and extraordinary joy
From the eve of my beginning my happiness she to employ.
To the one who blessed me with the mind and the desire
Learn from experience, use my strength to persevere.
To the one who listened, learned and bestowed unto me
A feeling to nurture, unchained my heart, set me free.
Who cradled my heart, wiped away the tears
From a broken soul and progressing fears.
To the one who I must help to understand
That there is clear water amidst the grains of sand
Each grain to be, a time we spend apart,

For now I gain strong will and an open heart.

K Williams

KEEP FIT!

It's Wednesday night and it's keep-fit night
And I wish I hadn't come.
I'm held in by yards of Lycra
With a thong-thing up my bum.

Find a space, form a line
I edge to the back and try to hide.
So how come I end up at the front
With slim bronzed beauties at each side.

I'm jumping and I'm skipping
My head is throbbing, my ears have popped.
I'm hopping and I'm bouncing
Why is my stomach still moving when I have stopped?

3

My face is red and flustered
I'm feeling tired and weak.
I'm sweaty, hot and sticky
And my incontinence is starting to leak.

My friends have made me come here
They all said that I should.
But how come I'm feeling so tired
When this is supposed to be doing me good.

So I go home tired and weary
But then my heart begins to sing
When my boyfriend looks at me and says
'Come here, you sexy, firm-bodied thing'.

So maybe there's a reason to exercise
But for me it's not easy to tell.
All that skipping and jumping and running
To me is sheer bloody hell.

Ruth Duckels

NON-SMOKERS

When I go out I like to smoke
but there's a group of people who pretend to choke
Coughing, spluttering, it's in my eyes
Constant moaning, groans and sighs
Move your fag it's intolerable
I can't stand the smell it's really horrible
Reformed smokers are the worst
sit with them and you've been cursed
You don't argue or move your lips
or they'll blast you with their quitting tips
They come round my house, complain about the smell
then *Why don't you leave!* - I try not to yell
Will they shut up, will it ever cease?
just let us smokers *die* in *peace.*

Marcia Tanner

4

TRUE FRIENDS

True friends are there for you in need,
Giving advice on the life you lead,
Letting you do as you please,
Making you feel safe and at ease.

True friends are there to listen to you,
They understand and try to help too,
Breaking the problems down as one,
To make way, and have some fun.

True friends care and trust one another,
Just like the relationship between son and mother,
Never too close, but always near,
To help shed away those fears and tears.

Debbie Avery

UNTITLED

My favourite time is when I dream
Night and day, so it would seem,
All the things I want to do
I can make them all come true.

The perfect man who's in my mind
Can be fun, but also kind,
He would never hurt me though
Not like ones I really know.

My body I can give for free
See only what I want to see,
I don't have to heed a warning
With a bad head in the morning.

You should see me sing or dance
I always get a second glance,
The admiration's there to keep
When I try to get to sleep.

I know that I am in control
Like a film, I cut and roll,
In situations I'm on song
In my eyes I do no wrong.

I could live my life in bed
Keep the truth out of my head,
But fantasy it can be lonely
When you are your one and only.

Viki Brice

I WAIT

I wait,
for the phone to ring, a letter through the post, a knock at
the door, a meeting in the street.

Maybe you have lost my address, can't find my phone number,
or just forgotten me.

I walk where we walked,
your name crops up in my conversation, now and then.
My thoughts, when alone often wander to you, I read your letters
when nothing else to do.
I remember your smile, which made me smile, but have you
forgotten?

Were they lies you told me, to make me feel better, to shut me up,
to keep me quiet and happy, spur of the moment lies?

Did you tell me anything that was true, or are they just forgotten
lies?

The way you touched me, looked at me, held me, said that you
wanted me forever.

Do you remember?
I wait to forget.

Julia Blake

THE REC

Sometimes when I feel troubled
I like to visit the park.
Here I can leave all my worries behind
Becoming the child in my heart.

Of course, it's changed since I was young,
I used to come here, as a treat,
I'd play ball games on the grass
And sometimes see young lovers meet.

They've taken away the slide,
And paint's peeling off the swings,
The roundabout has also gone,
Vandals dismantled the bins.

Yet still I venture here
To gather my thoughts alone,
I watch today's little ones
Until the day comes to a close.

Angela Mills

HAMPSHIRE

Hampshire is a splendid county,
Rolling downs and mighty towns,
Villages in sheltered valleys,
Where in rivers fish abound.

Westward look to Port Southampton
Mighty docks and strong old walls,
Ancient Romans knew its harbour
Was protection from the storms.

To the eastward there is Pompey
Known by sailors everywhere,
Specially placed in my affection
For in childhood I lived there.

7

Titchfield has a grand old abbey,
Bishops' Waltham Palace grounds,
Portchester its famous castle,
On the hill forts can be found.

Splendid is our own New Forest
New! Good gracious, there's a laugh
Conqueror William he did plan it,
Mighty trees and bridle paths.

Living in this lovely county
I am happy to recall,
Visits to so many places
I must say, I love them all.

Kathleen Crawshaw

STILL WATERS RUN DEEP

The calm, smooth, silent water
Was moved by the dark stone.
A surface-destroying missile,
Thrown with careless intent,
Disturbed its facade and
Plunged deep into its liquid centre,
Causing an undulating ripple
Seemingly eternal.

Disordered water thought
It would never, never settle;
Contact with the smooth, dark
Heavy stone, had caused sensations,
Unlooked for and unusual.
Recreated an old longing;
To be a sparkling stream
Rushing headlong

Over the rocks, and down to meet
The glorious river, magnificent
And strong; pushing itself out
Into the uninhibited ocean:
But the stone sank to the bottom
And settled into the soft mud.
The ripples faded to a deception
Of serenity, but the deep, still,
Silent water would always remember
Its passing.

Judith Gay

HANGOVER CITY

Head throbbing like a generator
stomach churning like a cement mixer
eyes needing matchsticks
let me sleep another week.

A strange twist of fate
that the morning after
should reflect nothing of the jollities
of the merry night before.

Don't let me smell alcohol
or even sight a pub
just dig me a hole
away from lights and noise
where I can hide away
and attempt to feel human.

It really isn't fair
that I should feel struck down
simply because I drank a lot
and spent a night in town.

Abigail Goswell

RE-UNION

I haven't seen you all for so long
even though you're just on the end of the phone
life has got in the way
and before you know it you've aged as well.

Then you get to wondering about
how old friends are, how they've turned out
how things used to be
when we giggled together in groups.

Oh, how do I look?
I was thinner then
didn't have that double chin
could walk
without holding my belly in.

Will my achievements
pale against theirs?
Our lives have took so many turns
except mine has seemed to stand still
and moving on has been a battle of will.

I'll walk in there
with my head held high
things haven't been that bad
I'm still alive!

Evlynne Opomu

SAME LOVE FROM DIFFERENT PLACE

I love you,
you love me,
we hope that
this
will always
be.

10

There's someone
else,
that we forgot,
he loves us both
an awful lot!

No-one knows,
how it must
be,
to love
someone,
as much as
he.

He cannot tell
us,
in loving words
but we should
know,
and understand,
as we listen to
his loving *purrs*.

George Ponting

OUR ISLAND

Surrounded by sea our isle so serene
Its beauty in miniature reigns supreme.
Folks tired and weary from cities large
Succumb to its enchantment - no mystical mirage.

Picturesque thatched cottages, villages define
Rambling roses in gay profusion on walls entwine.
The added distinction of symbolic downs
Linking small contrasting towns.

11

The colourful harbours gentle breezes embrace,
Yachts, sails unfurl, their beauty adds grace.
Amidst this scene of glorious colour,
Boats large and small, in the lapping-tide anchor.
The towering cliffs, sheltered sandy beaches,
Are magically incorporated on this paradise of vistas.

Authors and poets of great renown,
Dwelt here, found inspiration, peace and calm.
Osbourne House, a landmark of historic reference,
Where Queen Victoria once graced her regal presence.

Seldom are nature's forces distressing,
Indisputable the many blessings.
Like a magic spell casting, its charm enfolds,
This Island of Wight - with power us holds.

Magdelena Hill

THE WAY TO ALVESTONE

Walk the way to Alvestone, through Ninham and Scotchell's Bridge
Pass ragged-robin, yarrow, may and wild rose hedge
Cross the road for Alvestone, stroll down the old Lea Lane
Where dock and nettle tangle with bracken and woody-bane
Rest awhile in Alvestone, by the river's edge
Where foxgloves spire and small gnats choir among the reedy beds
The mill once turned at Alvestone
And boats plied up the river -
Now a grassy breeze wafts through the wheel to set the
                              leaves a-quiver
There's brown fish in the water - rippling circles in the shade
Come - walk with me to Alvestone
To Mother Nature's glade.

G Sydney-Allen

BEACH HUTS

They huddle there like homeless tramps abandoned in the rain
And dream of laughing kids in shorts when summer comes again.
Capri and *Tide's View*, *Sunny Rest*, their names ironic now
When lashing waves attack the prom, as winds and tides allow.
Peevishly hurling *tracer* sand, or barrages of stones
Against the weathered peeling doors whose every timber groans.
And dinghies, tackle, lobster-pots, encroach round dampened feet
Content to hibernate a while through fog and rain and sleet.
Where grudgingly, the stalwart soul, well-wrapped, with head bent
down
Drags past, in tow, some hapless hound, to defecate or drown
As driving rain conspires to rust each padlock, bolt and hinge
Whilst windblown droplets mark the paint with abstract taint and
tinge.
Unwanted stains to scrub away as spring proclaims once more
An end to *stormforce* moods, with far more gentle seas in store.
Some feel the vandals ripping hurt; insults from dog or bird
They see it all, they hear it all, yet utter not a word.
So more nails here, fresh timber there. Some coats of bright new
paint
The tramps shake off the lethargy of winter's harsh restraint.
Their names take meaning once again, on beach huts dandified
That greet the passing crowds without; the family fun inside.
As bleach-white gulls cry overhead, and beach balls bounce below,
The prom's transformed, that skulked in gloom, a few brief months
ago.
It's strange how quickly, helped by man, the seasons change a
scene,
Those winter huts with scowls so glum, now smile with summer's
sheen.

R J Bradshaw

13

HAMPSHIRE

I have lived in Hampshire all of the time,
First in the country, but the town is fine,
The town has lots to do and is a great place,
But a countryside walk helps get out of the rat race!
There's walks by rivers and strolls by canals,
Walks through cornfields amongst the hay bales,
Basingstoke is the town I am in now,
It is why you never see a cow,
But Odiham and King John's Castle are not far away,
You should take a trip out there, visit it some day,
There are cinemas, ice rinks and restaurants nearby,
But I want some peace, I hear you cry.
On the John Pinkerton barge you could ride,
Have your picture taken, show it off with pride,
If you visit the country there are deer running free,
They really are there for you all to see,
My three children have heard talk of moving away,
But we want to stay here, is what they say,
They dance, play football and one is a scout,
There are many more activities I have no doubt.
I was born in Hampshire and do not want to move away,
And my wish to be granted for that I will pray.

Linda S Hooker

LOOKING DOWN ON WHITECLIFF BAY

When I am feeling deep despair
My heart like a heavy stone,
I take down my coat from off the peg
And prepare to walk alone.

I walk along the clifftops
As the wind blows through my hair,
And slowly, very slowly
The world begins to care.

For as I stand upon the peak
Looking down on Whitecliff Bay,
Each gusting breath of air
Sweeps unhappiness away.

And as I gaze upon the land
My world becomes anew,
For I cannot fail to be uplifted
So magnificent the view.

I watch the great waves crashing
As they pound upon the shore,
And feel a passion, for this island
For its beauty, and much more.

Then I turn again to battle
Against the wind and rain,
But know that I am ready
To face the world again.

Mary Ralph

THE LONELY SWAN

A beautiful, graceful, stately pair,
They made a majestic sight,
Silently gliding still waters, where
Their plumages mirrored pure-white.

The batches of four they strove to rear
All left them when fully grown
I tried to detect a falling tear
As their young ventured out alone.

And yet I felt they would be consoled,
For they were a lifelong pair,
But who will console just one, grown old,
Now swimming - so bravely - who'll care?

Grace Leeder-Jackson

15

HAMPSHIRE

A county full of lovely things
The forest heath and river brings
Great beauty and the rolling sea
Which flows along can only be
To bring great ships from far and wide
Upon the morn and evening tide
The village life of farm and home
And meadows where the cattle roam
Cathedral, churches, markets call
And modern things to please us all
The downland wonder wanders wide
With harebells blue
And by their side, grow
Flowers small of brilliant hue
So what to say in words so few
About a place so old, so new
It must be that at least for me
The one and only place to be.

Queenie Stevens

DEVON

'Tis lovely here in Devon,
With its cider and clotted cream,
Rose-covered thatched cottages,
Of which many people dream.

No rooster rules the farmyard,
No baby chicks around,
Pony and trap are forgotten
Baby lambs still abound.

Many hedgerows bulldozed down,
Less wildflowers to be found,
Fish in streams die of pollution,
Will there ever be a solution?

16

The EEC has wrecked our lives,
With their silly ridiculous rules,
Big diggers clean our ditches,
That man did better with tools.

We do still have the owls,
In the oak trees, hooting at night,
Their barns are now smart houses,
Which country folk don't think is right.

Mary Eveleigh

THOUGHTS OF THE HOUSEMAN STATUE IN BROMSGROVE

Please look at me as you pass by and then perhaps I'll know
the faces of the country folk I loved so long ago.
Oh happy half-forgotten days of innocence and joy,
the dreaming days of summertime when I was just a boy.
How gaily then I trod the lanes that run by Severn side,
and plucked life's offered favours from the spring at Whitsuntide
How winsome were the village girls I met at Bromsgrove Fair,
when gaslights flared and organs played brave steamy music there,
If only I could feel again the reins beneath my hand,
and hear the harness jingle over ridged and fallow land,
or tread with hobnailed measured tread the sunbaked cracking clay
along the banks of Willowherb that mark the Wychbold way.
Alas, it's only in your eyes that I hope now to see
reflections of the celandine and snowy damson tree.
So tarry here beside me, and then will sound again
the brazen note the stormcock cracked, the thrushes bell-like strain
across the river meadows where I can no longer roam
with joy to match the morning as I whistled my way home.
For only in your faces, and in your honest eyes
shall I hear the bells of Tardebigge and see the Severn rise.

Joan Shaw

17

MY LANCASHIRE

Factory chimneys, blackened smoke
Injured lungs, no mean joke;
Terraced houses in orderly rows
Gaslight flickers, a flame which glows.

A knocker-up with a lance of sound
To tap a window, on his cobbled round; ·
In storm or rain, just a tap will do
Wake up, it's time to toil anew.

Clogs and shawls, bowyanks tied tight
A dizzy head, a pint last night;
Hail smoggy morn, I go abroad
Clogs with irons spark the road.

The factory gates are opened wide
Alongside the cut where barges ride;
Shire-horses with a blaze of white
Brasses gleam in the early light.

Lancashire lasses in two's and three's
With pinnies on they laugh and tease;
I've got six rooms she's got four
A tackle - for her to keep the score.

Watch out now, for that picking stick
Suck that weft, and give a flick;
Another length of cotton cloth
Roll-on teatime, then I'm off.

Coalcarts blackened from hauling sacks
Coddy muck heaped in smelly stacks;
There's much to tell of Lancashire life
Sometimes beauty, sometimes strife.

But there is a Ribble and a Lune
Ha'penny Bridge where young ones spoon;
An old tram track to god-knows-where -
Lancashire, what memories there to share.
Jim Bland

UNTITLED

I had a dream when I lived in a city
That one day I'd escape to this county so pretty
Dorset, my treasure chest, gem of this isle
So steeped in history with tales of the past
Serenaded by birdsong as I sit on a stile
This is my home now, contentment at last.
The cawing of rooks, the bleating of lambs
Distant sound of a tractor but no traffic jams.
Down by the river with its gentle flow
I know a place where wild orchids still grow.
Thatched cottages in villages with quaint-sounding names
Smooth patch of green where children play games.
Tolpuddle and the martyrs known throughout the land
The sycamore tree still stands - where they met
A living memorial lest we forget.
I've seen the Cerne Abbas giant carved way up the hill
Who put him there, and why, puzzles me still?
Here, life is lived at a gentle pace
With time to explore I've meandered along to find Durdle Door.
A coastal wonder with arch of stone
Blue sky filled with gulls as I stand here alone.
I count my blessings then go on my way
Tomorrow I've plans for a different day
I'm going to visit Dorchester town
Where the dreaded Judge Jeffreys in wig and gown
Brought terror at the sound of his name
Now there's a tearoom named after him - what fame!
Dorset has beaches stretching for miles
I love watching children with their happy smiles
As they run to the sea, living in Dorset is heaven for me.

Edna Butler

THE COUNTRY CHURCHYARD

As I walk through the villages, I pass many churchyards
And it never fails to amaze me
That a place of such sorrow, possesses a beauty of its own
Each season brings its own loveliness
Adoring the tombstones in the miracle of creation
In autumn - a cloak of mist
Lingers like a ghostly shroud - enveloping the headstones
Its dewy moisture drops on the delicate dry leaves
Then suddenly - a slight breeze
Unlocks them from the parent tree
Causing them to flutter down
Nature's confetti, forming a rustling carpet on the ground
The winter's snow, neatly edges headstones
Or drifts - to cover inscriptions
And so for a while, all become unmarked and equal
In spring, up shoots the bulbs, so carefully planted
By the loved ones of those who are now gone
But never forgotten
The bare bone-like fingers of surrounding trees
Burst forth with green buds - then the leaves
Which gives camouflage to the feathered home builders
Who in turn - from nature's pulpit
Sing their song
The summer brings long shadows which fall across the graves
Giving shade to those who no longer feel the sun
Each plot abounds with flowers of many hues
Put there by relatives - who in their sorrow -
Fail to see
The beauty in the churchyard.

Jacqueline M Taylor

LEISURE

Gardening.
Working in my garden
Watching flowers grow
Hearing all the birdsong
Is so nice you know.
Camellias tall and healthy
Garlic, chives and parsley
Lavender and rosemary
Nuts, fruits and berries
Grass growing happily
And I am humming merrily
Whilst gardening at my leisure
And getting lots of pleasure.

A P F Gorman/Sandry

FEBRUARY

February is here with its promise of spring
The bulbs are showing and the birds start to sing
But beware winter is not over yet
The days can still be very cold and wet
So wrap up warm and mind how you go
Just in case we have that fall of snow.

February can be a happy time,
When words of love are put to rhyme
For it brings St Valentine's Day
Happy memories come to stay
So thank you God for the month of Feb
When many couples plan to wed
And when their marriage has begun
We wish them luck in years to come.

J A Booker

IT'S SPRINGTIME

A dreamy little dormouse,
Rubbed his tiny eyes one day,
And said *I must awaken,*
And so be on my way,
To get a tasty morsel,
Of lovely food to eat,
My paws are really very cold,
And so are my poor feet.
A meal would be most welcome,
Because for some time now,
I've slept so very deeply -
I really don't know how.
My bed is so uncomfy,
I must have dreamed a lot,
But I just can't remember,
How in this state I got.
He put his best foot forward,
And breathed the breath of spring,
How glad that I'm awake he said,
I've had a long lie-in!

Paula Hagan-Smith

UNTITLED

Gleaming sun
Warm breeze
Birds singing in the trees
Daffodils bursting out of their buds
Standing like soldiers in bright
Yellow hoods
Blue sky, bright and clear
Summertime is almost here.

Nicola Richardson

DALBY FOREST

To Dalby Forest we like to go
No matter the weather, sun, rain, wind or snow,
There's lots of walks for us to follow;
Be it over a ridge or down in a hollow.

As you enter the forest you pay a toll
It is for the car not for a stroll,
The visitor centre is a must
For information you can trust.

There's lots to be seen if you look around
Up in the trees and on the ground
So why not visit a forest near you
As there's lots of exciting things to do.

Mary Massey

THE BEACH

The wave broke, and I turned.
Faded memories fled - I don't know where.
That distant summer I had learned,
Of a land beyond compare.

The beautiful sunset warmed me,
Yet the saddening coldness clung.
Beside that gentle, silent sea
A silent shadow sung.

An empty beach - worked and used,
Serene - my rare release.
The security, the freedom,
Sacred haven of peace.

Vanessa Reeves (15)

23

THE GAMBLER

It flashed past the post at 20-1
and with it my money, my last hope had gone
I'd been there all day, now I couldn't go home
I stood there despondent, dejected, alone
A fistfull of money when I started out
Today I would win, of that I'd no doubt
But life has a habit of grinding you down
So I stood there again, the bookmaker's clown
Kept telling myself it's a wonderful life
Now I must pay the piper, go home to the wife
Ranting and raving, I'll get nothing for tea
Why did she marry a fool such as me?
Then comes the throwing of teacups and things
Oh what a miserable life gambling brings
When I say I'm sorry, this just makes her worse
She screams and she howls out a terrible curse
Tomorrow's the day, I have it worked out
She stifled my pleas with an almighty clout
You're senseless and gormless, you have no use
I could get her locked up, for husband abuse
Next morning I set off, full of intent
Hands tucked in my pockets, also the rent
I'll show her who's stupid, and can't back a winner
When I get my winnings, I'll treat her to dinner
They're under starter orders, now running round the track
This is it, it's too late now, can't get my money back
Number 10 is my horse, Piggot has the ride
And if I could I'd be there, sitting at his side
The bleeder's lost, and I am done, I don't possess a cent
My future, cardboard city, or living in a tent.

A W Nolan

UNTITLED

Now the working day is done it's time to rack my brain,
Then off into my own small world I wonder off again,
Sometimes I like to daydream sometimes I like to run,
Sometimes I like to play a joke it's all just harmless fun.
But most of all my passion, some people may find strange
I'm off into my garage to sit and rack my brains.

There she stands before me her paint a brilliant red,
Her engine clean, her body mean, sends wild thoughts through my
Head, the freedom she provides me as I hear the engine roar
I've never had this feeling and now I just want more.

The road flies by so quickly, a smile comes to my face,
I feel a love down deep inside I'm in another place.
So through the moonlit valleys I sit my legs astride
The engine roars beneath me I'm sure man's born to ride.

Ian Blevins

ODE TO HARRY

I'm not sure that it's a hobby
But it takes up a lot of my time
How to be a pal, a servant or slave
What's this, I hear you asking
Is this paid work or not?
Job satisfaction? Yes, it's got a lot.

What's this, I hear you asking
That could cause a person to grieve
Losing a sense of purpose
When the job is no longer there
The work is time-consuming
And by way of payment there's the odd purr.

If you've not guessed it yet
There's nothing else to say
It's being owned by a cat
There's nothing better than that.

C B Blythin

THE HOUR

I have this hour every day
In which I travel far away,
It could be just to the village shop
Or to dizzy heights of a mountain-top!
Today, it was hot Bombay
Tomorrow? - Well, who can say?

It's just one hour of sheer bliss
Like hungry touch of a lover's kiss,
Just sixty minutes before the kids come home
The ironing's finished, I've unplugged the phone,
Sometimes I travel back in time
To when the weather was always fine.

Back to childhood. Happy days!
Joyful, in so many ways!
How I wish we could recreate
That certain time, place and date,
When life was always glorious spring
A wonderful, innocent, easy thing.

I think about mankind at peace.
Will this burning hatred, ever cease?
It envelops our hopes, our joys and fears
With wars, pestilence and pitiful tears,
All of these things are within my power
Sorted and settled in just one hour!

Marie Mason

1984 - 1994 (DECADE OF DECADENCE
THE GROWTH OF SURROGATE MOTHERHOOD)

They took her baby away from her;
Taken from a swollen milk-filled breast,
Removed from the external womb of motherhood
To Ostermilk and an artificial place to rest.

The mother, deafened to plaintiff cries,
Packed her suitcase and moved from her bed
To her, now temporary, semi-detached suburban house
Soon to be exchanged for one better, she said.

And next year, when all's back to the norm,
She'll pack her suitcase and move in again,
To give birth to yet another squeeze-me, see-me-cry doll
To be sold for enough dollars, pounds or yen.

Oh daddy, where's my real mummy now?
Why she's somewhere across the sea,
Discussing contracts for babies she's willing to sell,
But whose souls she gives away free.

And in this supermarket of gleaming white
Row upon row of antiseptic plastic carriers hang in view,
Why not have a black one this time?
There's a special offer on two!
Do you want them gift wrapped and sent
Or will you take them with you?

B D Daniel

MY WORLD

My God! What are you doing?
Don't you know what's going on?
You stand there smug on your Persian rug
And tell me there's nothing wrong.

27

You'd like me to keep silent
While you flush my world down the drain,
This may make you blue but I've got news for you,
You had better think again.

You fill my seas with your toxins
And cut my trees from the land,
You won't be glad till all the water's bad
And the earth's been turned to sand.

What good will your money do you
When your children come to see
The blackened waste of your distaste
That is their legacy.

And when my world's a cauldron
And you proudly stand and gloat,
May your soul despair fighting for some air
In hell's hot and fiery moat.

Christopher Holland

BEGGAR

Have you any change, sir?
Please spare me 50p,
But sir, I'd give to you, sir,
If I was you and you were me.

Please spare me 50p, sir,
So I can get food to eat,
I slept out here last night, sir,
Out here on this street.

I'm not a public nuisance, sir,
Well, I don't mean to be,
Sir, I'd be so grateful
If you could spare me 50p.

Adrian Dowrick

A RECKONING

Twenty years ago Johnnie wore his hair unnaturally bald
Joined a youth club called National Front
And ruled the street with his brother's gang
Stuffing his pockets with crime and their opinions;
Their bulldog tattoos, blood-red laces
And matching braces
Supported Blues when they played at St Andrews,
Discovered his roots, man, put on his Doc Martin
Boots, man,
Shoved a blade into a black boy's back, man,
Whose mother scrubbed floors at the General Hospital
And father drove buses around the capital.

But them twenty years have gone, man,
And Johnnie with good shoes and naturally bald
Catches the bus with a pain in his chest
To the hospital where his wife cleans the toilets
And the black doctors know all the best cures.

Paul Waight

SOCIAL EVENT OF THE YEAR

Spending hours in front of a mirror at home
Making sure you look just right.
Speaking to everyone you know on the phone,
To see what they're wearing tonight.

Seven o'clock and the time is right,
To set off out the front door.
This is it . . . the big night!
The one you've been waiting for.

You can hear the noise loud and clear
From the other end of the street.
People arriving with cases of beer,
Presents and morsels to eat.

29

Greeted by the host, your friendly hello's
Are swallowed by the noisy throng.
You see someone you actually know
Dancing to your favourite song.

The music is loud enough to break the glass,
And to crack the doors.
Sitting with friends, having a laugh
And a break from the dance floor.

Everyone's eating peanuts and treats
From bowls around the place.
Most of them end up down the back of the suite
Or smeared on a portrait's face.

At the end of the night, about half-past-one
The place is a terrible mess.
But everyone has had brilliant fun
Parties are simply the best!

Nicola Baughan

FIXING

I'll go
When the day wakes
I'll leave
When the night lifts
Slip into the warm frosted morning
From the cold steamy bed.

I'll try
Not to wake you
Not to let you know
I was there
Right beside you
Your face turned away.

I won't
Stay much longer
Just a few minutes more
And you'll never see
You were there
Right inside me
Your mind led astray.

Stephanie Morris

GROWING-UP

Many grown-ups seem to humiliate
While others leave you to fate.
Growing-up comes to those who wait
But now they aren't allowed to.

They dress you up when you are small
In clothes which make you look tall.
They give you your life but move it on
At such a speed it feels wrong.

You aren't allowed to play
And each and every day,
They educate your mind to
Opinions which are their own.

Some never grow up to adulthood
Some others wish they would.
But it is childhood which keeps
People hoping, playing and entertaining,
Like I wish I could.

Melissa Pollard

INAMORATA

Passion is rising within me
Like fires after the drought,
Sweeping through my body,
Like ripples of endless silk.
My spirits are soaring,
And my mind is reeling,
When faced with this blinding red.
The sunlight is glaring,
As the heat is overpowering,
Whilst my body yearns for thee.

My love is as sweet
As peace after war.
It is as selfless
As it is helpless.
I am happy, yet sad,
Lonely, yet not alone,
Suffocating, yet free to be.
Drowning in emotions
You have stirred in me,
Setting me free.

I am attracted to you,
Like sight to the blind,
And water to the thirsty.
My heart no longer is mine,
For it is under the power of thine.
I live my life,
If only to give it to thee.
Your presence to me,
Is like the stars in the sky -
Eternal, unending, and sent from on high.

Nicola Young

ODE TO ALL CHECKOUT OPERATORS!

'Good morning madam.' 'How are you sir?'
This language of a checkout girl, causes not a stir,
These such polite greetings, we so often use
To them they are courteous, but to us they amuse,
Quite often our presence is simply ignored
Until they need help 'cause the ice-cream has thawed,
Seen as a fixture, a body but no brain
We're stupid, or braindead, or perhaps just insane,
So it gives me great pleasure, when I'm able to tell
I'm doing three *A Levels*, and I'm doing quite well.

Attached to my uniform for all to see
Is my own name-badge, but how can this be?
If this is my name, why do people persist
To call me love, darling, sweetheart or miss?
But for the while I'll continue to sit
Smile sweetly and greet you, with my charm and my wit,
You see the life of a checkout girl, well, it's the bees' knees
'Come on, move along, next customer please.'

Clare Jones

YARMOUTH MARSHES

Desolation is more than words -
but wind across the marshes
nears

Sea salt cakes the rushes' stems
while wrecks of boats lie couched in mud for
years

Even peace is ominous
the whir of wind, the cry of bird
fears

33

A curlew cheats across the flats,
far wave boom the lonely sound it
hears

Tense stillness haunts this place -
this land on which the sea lays its
tears.

Jean Newnham

MY DORSET

Now Dorset is a lovely place
In which I do reside
My childhood days which were spent here
I recall with great pride
The lovely lanes in which I strolled
In spring when leaves were green
Which in the autumn turned to gold
Made such a pretty scene
And when the summer sun shines down
On Dorset's golden sand
To take a walk along the shore
Makes me feel really grand
And so I'll add just one more thing
I never will deny
It's here in Dorset I was born
And where I hope to die.

J Knapman

HAMPSHIRE

What is Hampshire to me?
Hozeley I love, you see,
Plants grow there, I have seen,
You must not hurry, take your time.
There are so many, people will never know,
So many walks you can go,
Never, never go on your own,
It's not as safe as it used to be.
Somebody asks me, where is God?
That's where he'll be for me,
There are so many local walks,
Beauty that is given free.
Stately homes you can go,
They are mostly for show,
Drive to the New Forest, leave your car,
You can walk so far.
Hampshire's got so much to offer,
If only you went to explore,
Why not go to the Greywell Canal?
You will see birds of every kind,
You will see more at nesting time.
Nature Walks have grown much more,
Gives me so much to explore,
I am an OAP now, you see,
Hampshire means so much to me.
I don't think it will stay the same,
I have seen such a change.

Roma Cooper

MY WALES

I have lived in Wales for all of my life
It is more than home to me,
I was born here, a child, then as a wife
It's my love for the place you see.

Many feet once trod this mossy old floor
Of a chapel you can see,
The road up to the entrance door
Is high with greenery.

The grass grows green, and very tall
And no-one worships there at all,
Windows are smashed, as you'd expect
Just a sample of modern neglect.

Folk now worship just the same
Not always in chapel, most will claim,
They watch TV and join the throng
And thank the Lord in prayer and song.

Land Of My Fathers, that is the choice,
Of song today; in loud, rude voice,
Where daffodils bloom in sun and in shade
And the mighty Red Dragon strides out unafraid.

Choirs echoing down o'er valleys and hills
Man conquering heights, forgetting all ills,
He stands and he gazes, from the peak, aghast
Beauty for ever, views unsurpassed.

The rocks they have stood the test of time
Tipped on edge against the skyline,
The peaceful quiet, the squawk of a bird
This is paradise, *have you not heard?*

Evelyn Goldsmith

GETTING UP

Well, Pat, it's not what I thought it would be,
I wake up in the morning, turn back the
Eiderdown, then the sheet and blanket, we
Hold on to the sides of the bed, feel free.

Sit up, hold one leg at a time, and place
Feet gently on the floor, sit on a seat,
Rub my knees and feet with a cream, not face
Then pull socks over feet and legs, complete.

Don knickers and then long trousers, I do
Top half is now started upon; cream now
On my shoulders and hands are rubbed into,
Then on with brassiere, fastening how!

Arms through straps of vest and somehow pulled down
And next on a blouse buttoned up down the front;
To do up, o'er the top a cardigan
Done up at the front with buttons to hunt!

Try to lift up with two hands on the chair
Pivot around and sit on my wheelchair,
Turn and look in the mirror to comb hair
Pat, combing back of my hair with great care.

Swivel around and Pat put on my socks
Struggle in some shoes and push down the toes,
Tie a granny knot, then look at the clocks -
Saying *time for breakfast,* anything goes.

G M Albon

A KIMBERLIN'S PARADISE

Over thirty years ago I left the city's smoke
and wandered down to Weymouth by the sea.
I left old friends behind me and family I loved dear
to seek a new life where I might be free.

In the city I had dreamed of living by the shore
where sun and sand and air were fresh and clean.
Where the seagull's plaintive cry would echo on the wind
and kindle thoughts of things that might have been.

But in Dorset I found more than in my fairest dreams.
The rolling hills and heathland stark and wild.
Gentle streams that softly flow unhurried to the sea
and rocky coves that smugglers once reviled.

I have wondered at the sweep of Chesil's pebbled arc.
At Portland's Isle where men have quarried stone.
And at Dorset's county town where Hardy's heart was laid
and Maiden Castle's ramparts stand alone.

Villages that nestle low between the rolling hills
where peace and quiet abound on summer days.
Churches that for centuries have opened wide their doors
and echoed down the years with songs of praise.

Spaniards bold once sailed the seas with dreams of conquest
spurred,
and Roman Legions marched with swords and shields.
Tudor Kings built fortresses to guard against the foe,
and brave men sailed for D-Day's battlefields.

There are treasures here for those who seek a gentler life
more precious yet than those of which I spoke.
But the greatest of them all is that I cherish most,
The kindly hearts and minds of Dorset folk.

Peter Yates

THE WARM COMFY CHAIR

My Grandmother is dying, getting ready to leave,
Going somewhere which I can't perceive,
But leaving her husband and her warm comfy chair;
I believe in heaven, so I suppose she'll go there.

But she's leaving us for it and just going somewhere,
It's not somewhere I can envisage like her warm comfy chair.
They've always lived there in that house of theirs,
Doing their chores and sharing their cares.

Life did not exist before that warm comfy chair,
The town just exists because they still live there.
She was indestructible and just always there,
So now though she's going, we'll remember her . . . there.

Rosalyn Carr

ENGLAND

England the isle I hold most dear,
Although I travel far and near
No place can match for me
My isle surrounded by sea.

The contrasts which abound,
Could never be found
In multitude, as they are here,
In my little island so dear.

City and country side by side,
The golden beach by the incoming tide,
The sun, then rain; the heat, then cold
England, the land of contrasts unfold.

Green fields then rocky moor and fell
Mountain streams, a sunlit dell
Oak woods, pine woods, sun then storm,
I thank God I was England born.
Peter Hynes

TEARS

They trickle like a summer stream;
Shining like stars at night as they flicker
through the light, down the side of our face,
as a stream flowing down the mountainside.
Tears not of joy, but of sorrow.
Sorrow of losing someone, special to ourselves.
maybe not forever, but for a while.
The sorrow of not having someone to hug
when you need hugging,
Or someone to be kissed by, when you need kissing.
Maybe I'd fallen, not like the tears on my face,
but fallen deep - into a pool -
A pool of love.

J Loader

LOVE 'EM AND LEAVE 'EM!

Why did I allow myself to fall so deep,
knowing full well, it was only for weeks.
Four weeks of blistering passion, desire, adoration,
why did I promote this exploration.
Did I not realise the numbness of the aftermath,
the bleary-eyed path, void of sparkle and wanderlust,
my whole perception has now gone bust.

I picture my lover, my eyes begin to well, there's so
much I want to tell.
Melancholic memories unleashed from my brain, the
nostalgia slowly drives me insane,
Amorous clinches strobe my mind then gradually
disperse into tide and are carried away far out to
sea only to be washed up and rebuked at me.

Charlotte Ford

THE GLASTONBURY MUSIC FESTIVAL

If you're into music
You must come down
To the festival of the year
Here in Glastonbury town.

The hippies their jiving
All through the day
To bands like the Lemonheads
Nirvana and Suede.

The locals they hate it
The noise and the mess
But who gives a toss
'Cos this festival's the best.

Many tents are set-up
But no-one will sleep
'Cos everyone's headbanging
And stomping their feet.

But tomorrow and dusk
All will come to a close
We'll then pack up our things
And go home I suppose.

Pippa Drake-Lee

TOGETHER AGAIN?

You've left me sad and all alone
After knowing how close we'd grown,
Side by side we laughed, we'd cried
Before the painful way you died.

I stopped awhile beside your grave
A breath of life to me you gave,
I whispered things I wished I'd said
Over the earth, now your bed.

I kissed the rose before it fell
Upon your body I knew so well,
Day by day I'll think of you less
As I sort my life out of this mess.

I'll visit you each starry night
And tell you that I'm feeling all right,
Flowers now are all I can give
For you are dead and I still live.

A part of me just died that day
In a veil of gloom my hope lay,
I remember you in youthful bliss
Cherished memories of our lasting wish.

Hopes and dreams and wishes gone
It's you I want, I wish for none,
My life's a game of solitaire
It's lonely here, I just don't care.

Now there is just one escape
For suicide is heaven's gate,
I'll open it carefully to ease the pain
Never to look back again.

Clare Davison

THE GARDEN IN SUMMER

I am sitting in the garden
Scratching from head to toe,
Midges and greenfly surround me
I can hear things buzzing too.

But although I'm being eaten
I really must confess,
I do enjoy the garden
In spite of all the pests.

I love the morning freshness
The scents and butterflies,
The spiders' webs among the flowers
The ever-changing skies.

The splashing of the fountain
As it falls among the leaves,
In the pond that lures the dragon-flies
With their beautiful azure gleam.

And in the summer evening
When the garden's cool and still,
The heat of the day forgotten
And the bird song just a trill.

One looks at the beauty around one
Petals closed on another day,
And know that God has been working
In His very special way.

Olive Curtis

A DORSET VILLAGE

A place of enchantment, a place to dream
Full of thatched cottages, banked by a stream
As I walk past the church, I survey it in awe
If it's peace you are seeking, you could ask for no more.

I continue my journey through footpath and grass
As sheep and their lambs wander happily past
The scenery changes with surprising ease
The next thing you see is the beach and the sea.

The people are also a breed apart
They are friendly and warm, with a kindness of heart
If it's help that you need, they will all lend a hand
A village in Dorset, is the best in the land.

Margaret Hankin

STORMY WEATHER

Promises were made, when sea was blue
Waves of passion, no longer true,
Heaven's rain down upon my back,
I face the sky
It turns black.

The yellow sands, strewn with waste
Seagulls squawking, dive to taste,
Ships are sighted, out to sea,
Leaving their spillage
Our misery.

Loud thunder rolls, so much pain
Lightning strikes, no not again!
Stormy weather, drab darkened skies,
Through cloudy thoughts
There's always lies.

Sun never sets, upon the beach
There is hope, but cannot be reached,
Tides to crash, upon the shore,
It always rains
And forever pours.

Jenny Higgins

LOVE ON PEOPLE, PEOPLE ON LOVE

Why do people rave on about love as if we can't live without it?
Do they expect me to believe this silly myth?
I doubt it!
It's just their way of saying:
*I got stung too. But I'll pass on this senseless nonsense
to amuse you.*

There's plenty more fish in the sea.
Oh well! There you have it.
That's just fine if you're a crab or an eel.
Am I? Are you?
I doubt it!

If it's to be, it'll be.
Oh! Another pearl of wisdom.
Don't these people understand;
Nothing's ever that easy?
I doubt it!

They're not worth the trouble love.
Oh great, now Gran's joining in
With her tales of woe and tribulation
And of how love and sex are just silly notions.
Does she really think I want to hear about all that?
Well, no, I don't,
And I can't say, *I doubt that!*

Zoe Shaheen

SPRING

Spring's there all year
coiled in the ground
inside frosted beds
crusted and cold.

Then a throb of snowdrops mocks
drifts that have cleared.
Crocuses come, gush purple and gold,
seduce a shy sun to appear.

Now the beds move
in soft undulation, blent
in rhythmic joy.
Springs are silent.

Justin Barnard

WAVES OF FEAR

As the waves caressed the moonlit shore
she wiped a tear from her eye.
Why was life being so unkind to her?
The door to happiness must surely open soon, she thought.
Why had feelings of love and affection now turned to fears?
Relationships could be deceptive, like the moon's appearance
in the sky,
but obsessional thoughts had haunted her for years.
Could her dreams and desires ever come true?
Her heart cried out for reassurance.
She was clear about what she needed -
a warm blanket of emotional security
wrapped tightly around her frightened form,
comforting her with love, hope and purity.

Andy Blackwell

COUNTRY RETREAT

My house feels like a palace
It means so much to me
I never ever want to move
I like the view I see
When I glance out through the window
I see open space and peace
If I ever had to move from here
Tranquillity would cease
So I will try my very best
To keep my lovely home
Who knows, with a little luck
I will never have to roam.

Rose Froud

TIMEWARP

Pale shafts of light through threatening rainclouds drown
In pools of silver on the distant sea,
Beyond the sombre gorse and stunted tree
And long-dead bracken, winter brown.

Far hazy folds of hills in westering sun,
Where cliffpaths undulate by shingle shore
Lace-fringed, or lashed in wild winds' roar,
Deserted 'til their rage is done.

The grey-towered church through filigree of ash
With snowdrops 'neath bare branches carpeted,
While bourns, brimful in winter, chalk spring-fed
Old manor-house or moss-thatched cottage pass.

Soon, hedgerows wild in springtime, dripping white,
Banks startling with their early summer hues:
Lych-gates, rough churchyards, ancient yews
And swallows swooping in the evening light.

Then morning sunlight on the lynchetts green
And rounded barrows on the downland crest,
A buzzard soaring to its treetop nest;
A timeless, never-changing scene?

Space-age intruders on our summits stand
And watch with steely eyes as progress churns
The bluebell wood - then, concrete-laden, turns
To smother heath and copse and pastureland.

Seek out remaining beauty there for all to share
Despite destruction which each new age brings!
O'er ridgeway track the lark unheeding sings
While gulls flock seaward through the salty air.

Dena Sealy

SUMMER IN DORSET

Heedlessly they rush along
In a never-ending stream,
Cars of every size and shape
In the sunlight glint and gleam.

Let us leave the broad highway
And the lonely byways seek,
Till the peace and solitude
To our minds and spirits speak.

Wander on the purple heath
Where the gorse and heather grow,
By a gently murmuring brook
See the crystal waters flow.

'Neath the trees of varied hue
Standing slender, cool and tall,
Hear a cuckoo suddenly
Sound its clear familiar call.

Till once more we find ourselves
Mingling with the busy throng,
Taking with us memories
Of a blackbird's mellow song.

Jean E Bellamy

UNTITLED

Of all the counties in England
Hampshire is the best,
Its landscape and its history
A cut above the rest.

Think of the Abbey at Romsey,
Quaint, village churches to admire,
The ancient stones of Winchester,
Cathedral, close, and choir.

The Itchen, Test and Meon
Afford one much delight,
In all the seasons of the year
They are a lovely sight.

Gilbert White of Selborne,
Cobbett and Mitford too,
Florence Nightingale and Charlotte Yonge
Is to name but a few

Of Hampshire's great and famous
But to one we make special claim,
She lies at rest in Winchester,
Jane Austen is her name.

D W Symons

MY WINTER CREATURE COMFORTS

The hedgehog flattens himself to crawl under the garden gate
He fell in the garden pond getting a drink, I saved him before it
was too late.
His antics make me laugh
As he comes wobbling down the garden path.
The robin comes to visit us every year
It gives me such pleasure when his redbreast appears.
The blue-tits and yellow hammers
Feed off the seeds of the lilac tree,
The sparrow hawk dives down from the sky
Gives us the once-over with his beady eye,
The blackbirds stay here all of the year
The starlings send the cats fleeing with a peck on the ear,
Best of all come the frogs to spawn in the pond
With their croaking frog-song
So happy that spring is here and that the winter has gone.

E B Calder

THE PLACE-NAMES OF DORSET

In days of old when knights were bold
    The Dorset ladies liked it
And chaps with maps
    Sat down and told us all about it.
The names they chose were written down -
    A very fine collection
And to this day those place-names stay
    Remembered with affection.

When Romans had *dunroamin* 'round
    And found they liked the area
They settled down in Dorchester
    And called it Durnovaria.

On Ashmore pond, there's ducks and fowl
    And swans at Abbotsbury
Pigs were bred, or so it's said
    At Toller Porcorum, (not Blandford Forum)
While deer run free on Cranborne Chase
    It seems to be that kind of place.

From Old Harry Rock to Worbarrow Bay
    Your footsteps could lead you the ancient Priests' Way
By Durlston and Kimmeridge and Tilly Whim's Cave
    Past the quarries of Worth and Old Jesty's grave.

Then there's Minterne Magna, Mapperton, Morden
    Melbury Bubb and Maiden Newton,
We all know Wimborne, Wick, West Moors
    And Weymouth, Wareham and Wool.
    This list goes on for evermore,
I hope you're not finding it dull!

Edward E Oliver

LLYN BRIANNE RESERVOIR

There stood the blackened skeleton of a farmhouse husk
On the bank of a nearly dry reservoir
I enter the ruin. There's a chimney still, iron deep in rust
Where once had burnt a blazing log fire.
How long had the farming family been departed?
Newly housed and duly compensated
In some modern bungalow, but so downhearted
Living an alien life which they hated.
I wondered if the water in which their taps ran
Sometimes passed through the roofless room in which I was now?
Old and listless, they probably didn't give a damn
Preferring to dream of their drowned farm and favourite cow.

We return along a once-track sided with soaked stumps of oak
There, too, remained an old paled fence
And sodden ex-fields which could so many memories evoke
In those who remember twenty years since.
It will be a good thing when the rains come again
To cover progression's seeming madness
And fill the reservoir with waters serene
To obliterate the past scenes of sadness.

Marjorie Cooper

CYCLE YOUR TROUBLES AWAY

When I'm bored with life, or just had a particularly hard day,
i like nothing more than to climb on my bike and pedal away.
Sometimes it's five miles, or fifteen at the most,
I never know my destination, yet manage never to get lost.

I find it peaceful, relaxing not to mention good for the heart,
It helps me keep things together when all around me is falling apart.
Mostly I cycle on my own, but sometimes it helps to bring a friend,
I'm not saying it solves all my problems, but it provides a
                            happy way for me to contend!

Alexis Cameron

UNTITLED

I'm beginning to see the light
I can imagine people's plight
When they realise with fright . . .
Someone else could die tonight.
We all hope that someone sees
The hatred stirring in the trees
The victims begging *please* . . .
As well as praying on their knees.
When will we realise something's wrong
When all our friends have gone?
I wish they would go, the devil's spawn . . .
So our land can be as one.

Julie Ann Campbell

GROOVY PASTIMES

If you're feeling kind of bored
and don't know what to do,
one exciting pastime
is to buy some gum and *chew!*

Chewing's really groovy
and it sure makes you look cool!
And you'll remember all the stunts
you did with gum at school.

You can wind it 'round your finger
and pull it through your toes!
Or blow some *massive* bubbles
that *pop* across your nose!

You can stick it on the bedpost
at night when you're in bed,
and spend the next day chewing too
or read a book instead!

Emma Green

PARENTS

Parents are bossy
Parents are mean
Parents are nosy
And ask where you've been.
Parents are embarrassing
Parents can't dance
Parents keep talking
They don't give us a chance.
Parents will argue
From morning 'til night
There's never a moment
When parents aren't right.
Parents have nicknames
Like *snuggles* or *honey*
Parents can never
Find enough money.
Parents are loving
Parents are fair
Parents give kisses
Attention and care.
Parents are here
They won't go away
But I love my parents
So I do hope they stay.

Natasha Hockridge (17)

SANCTUARY

I know these hills,
these ordered fields
and ancient tree,
this race of yeoman
rooted here in time.
     I know them all
     and knowing, love.

53

I love these coasts,
these secret coves
and sprinkled farms.
This greeny dapple
of the early light.
      I love them so
      and loving, fear.

I fear that greed
will overwhelm
and violate
this cloistered union
of the land and men.
      I fear for them
      and fearing, hope.

I hope these heirs
to moor and sea
and rich red soil
will pledge their land
to those who follow on.
      I hope for this
      and hoping, pray.

I pray in death
to lie in peace
beneath these skies
beside familiar tors
among my fellowmen.
      And be at one
      with things I know.

H Davies

UNTITLED

Once a fortnight without fail
When my dole is due,
I get up really early
And make myself a brew.
Then, when I am dressed
And had myself a shave,
I go and cash my cheque
And promise Mum I'll save.
But the lure of the pub is always there
Every other week,
And when I smell the lager
My resistance is too weak.
I go with good intentions
Just a pint or two,
A pack of cigarettes
And a game of darts will do.
Then before I know it
Last order bells are ringing,
I've had a few too many
I know because I'm singing.
So now it's home again
To get myself some kip,
Preparing for the morning
No doubt my Mum will flip.
You only got your dole
Yesterday at ten,
It's taken just a day
To spend the lot again.

Christine Owen

GUILTY FEELINGS

Should I be here? Should I really be with you?
Is it right for me to say just how much I've missed you?
A voice inside my head is telling me to go,
to forget my dreams that I should always follow.
Although my heart always beats
more times than I can count,
more times it's hard to swallow
the guilt that's coming out.
I don't want to tell you that our togetherness will end
and maybe we should stay distant and you would be my friend.
I can't keep inside all my thoughts I hide
but how can I tell you what's happening to my mind.

Are we really here or is it just our dreams?
I wish we could drift to the bluest seas,
where no-one could ever find us,
we would be alone there, hiding from the whispers
and eyes that always glare.
But when I wake up to reality,
that I'm just something to you
for you to feel manly and take away your blues.

I feel so stuck now that I know I'm another one
who's there when she's not to repair the damage done,
or is it too late to undo this, have we fell too deep
or is this something we really want to keep?
Secrets, passion, lust, guilt or none?
It's your turn to throw the dice,
but I feel you've already won.

L A Butler

SOMERSET COUNTY

Down in deepest Somerset
A light shines so bright.
Is where the cider apples grow
Down in deepest Somerset.
Taunton is that light so bright
That's where they make the cider so.
There's lots to see and do
Down in deepest Somerset.
There's country walks abound
Then the seashore for kids a lot.
Down in deepest Somerset
There's Taunton town
Minehead and Bridgewater too.
There's fun to be had all around
Down in deepest Somerset.

D J Atkinson

UNREALITY

She scans her surroundings through a distorted lense
Exploring the tunnels of her sixth sense
As she tries to absorb the movement around her
Unreality is beginning to blind her
Look at that girl, I think she's insane
Unleashed in her own magical world again
But she's erasing all her pain
Subsiding in storm clouds, got nothing to gain.

His vision dances in a thousand lights
Distorted images that don't look right
His morals and values slowly pass by
Emotions and feelings, they wither and die
He shouted for help, but no-one came
Now shooting stars invade his brain
But for now, the world won't seem so cold
Amid this beautiful, fantasy world.
Jesica Cullen

57

THE RIDDLE OF DORSET'S CHESIL STRAND

Come on a mystical journey, along Chesil Bank
with sights never to forget,
Westward to a haven for birds,
that wonder of England's proud Dorset,
Stretches eighteen miles of mixed shingle,
where seapeas thrive and flower,
Walking over various pebble sizes,
enjoying magic within each hour.

Mute swans mass at Chesil's swannery,
dating from history's long past,
White surf swiftly rinsing stones,
tides ebbing and flowing so fast,
An anomoly in cliffed Dorset,
as sharp shelves rise off the beach,
Bubbling waters recede and swirl,
from a clear shore soon out of reach.

Sea terns with ringed plover,
fly in over Chesil once more to feed,
Dunlin with turnstone, follow oyster-catchers
and rummage among greenweed,
A small flock of redbreasted merganser,
dive deep and hunt for eel,
While those haunting cries of a whimbrel,
enlivens a scene so real.

As anglers cast for bass,
from a sloping shingled shore,
And Fleet's inland lagoon, runs alongside,
beckoning once more,
A narrow outlet running to the sea,
past flats of rich organic silt,
In late April parties of bar-tailed godwit,
mirrored across pale skies migrate and wilt.

The beautiful village of Abbotsbury,
amass with gardens of subtropical plant,
With a view of the Fleet and Chesil,
they are always worth a second glance,
Like a fairytale domain so fresh and verdant,
spreading majestically before your feet,
On a steep green backdrop of chalk downs,
fields of colour slope and meet.

Growing from bare shingle, a tiny myriad of flowers
stand in misty ashen light
While shrubs of lycium Chinese,
paints a picture of oriental sight,
An elemental place,
consisting of shingle, sea and sky,
As swirling roaring sou'westers,
pounds surf and waves straight by.

From the delicate laps and back gurglings,
of infrequent short dead-calms,
A beached zone of wetted pebbles,
adds a beauty and hypnotic charm,
With beaches of eerie stillness,
ahead they twist and lie,
An exquisite illusion like a golden ghost,
beckons from a pale-blue sky.

Jim Wilson

WAY, WAY

Way, way back in 1942
you both said *yes we do*
through the war your love grew strong
then along came little John.

Little John he was sweet
so 18 months later along came Pete.
He wasn't a girl so you did some sobbin'
A few years later along came Robin.

You thought you had your little gang
but many years later came Judith Anne.

And now your family was complete
life to you was oh so sweet
the children they soon did marry
they had their children, your name to carry.

Margaret Etherington

ONLY TONIGHT

My desire to be loved
is so strong, so very real
as my fingers gently caress
and stroke, and touch and feel.

The unity of body and soul
is one within my heart.
These sudden waves of passion
are tearing me apart.

As planets rise and planets fall
the music of love plays on.
I stop, I turn, I pause for breath
I've wanted this for so long.

It's been the perfect performance
for you and me alike.
I smile and I lower my flute
there will never be another tonight.

Tania Hales

LANE

Sometimes, we walk together,
You and I, Kismet,
Along a path of fading memory
Where briars of time
Tug gently at our clothes.
But always then we meet
That gate, jammed fast, immovable,
Invisible to everyone but us,
Which now we cannot climb.
Do you see, Kismet,
Outlines of a house, not built?
Do you hear echoes of a melody, unplayed?
Listen to the squealings
Of our children, still unborn.
Smell perfume of flowers
We have never found.
That is all thin news, Kismet,
From lands, where
We have never been.
But, one day, Kismet,
We shall go down that path,
Untrammelled by the briars.
And the gate will open
Into our magic distance.

Dean Juniper

MINE

When you're searching for someone,
faces whirl like a carousel
suspended in time,
The eyes you see, are they mine?

61

The face you see
is a deceptive reflection,
and words you don't say
prompt dumb introspection.
These thoughts take me
so far away
I am no longer here.

My eyes don't see you,
fickle illusion;
my hands don't touch you,
sweet confusion;
my ears don't hear you,
silent whisper;
For I am not here.

Then I look in your eyes
and I realise;
The eyes you see, can't be mine.

Alexandra Miller

DA BARMAN

Roll-up, roll-up, folks. Come and see
the greatest barman there will ever be,
he pours the pints better than anyone can
whether it be from a pump
whether it be from a can,
his Southern Comforts comforting
his Diamond Whites so pure,
and underneath he is too
of that I can be sure.
There are just two words
which make me tremble at the knees
it's when he leans over the bar
and says in his husky voice,
Yes please?

Hayley Swatridge

SISTERS

We have our laughs
we have our fights
but at the end of the day
we hug each other tight.

For we have always been close
like sisters should
even though we really have had
our feuds.

For I have always wanted
to see you're okay
no matter what time of day
to show I care and I'll always be there
no matter what.

For I hope you now see how much
you mean to me
from past, present and to an eternity.

Nicola Long

NEVER MIND

So many things you might have done
to save my life
but instead you shook your head
and said 'How sad.
Never mind'.

You chose to stare
into my all-white eyes
for just sufficient time to well
the driest of tears
and then you drew your line,
your lovely hand on mine,
shaking your pretty little head.
'Never mind'.

Open-mouthed, you receive the good news
that I'd drowned in the well of your tear.
In pity you mourned,
'I could do no more'
but my idea of a ghost screams *liar!*
And now I pass my time weaving indelible rhyme
on the worn lid of your eyes.
With my famous last line, your death echoes mine
and I chuckle, 'How sad.
Never mind'.

Darren Peers

REALITY

Laughter fills the crowded room,
outside the night is full of gloom.

She left the party after consuming much wine,
oblivious to committing any crime.
Along the country lanes she sped -
the drink having gone straight to head.
She did not see the man step out
until it was too late - she heard his shout.
Shock and drink confused her mind,
a dream? Reality? - The police car pulled up behind.
Soon she was in a haze of flashing blue lights,
she could hear muffled voices and the reading of
her rights.

In the dreary cell, sober now,
she repeatedly asked herself, *how, how, how?*
The accident was unclear
due to drink, or maybe fear.
Even drink failed to dissolve one thought within
her head -
The man, his pale face - he was dead.
Did he have children? Pets? A wife?
All she knew was that she'd taken away his life.
Beth Manley

THE BOTTLE

He seized me by my slender neck
I could not call or scream
He dragged me to his diningroom
where we could not be seen
he stripped me of my flimsy wrap
and gazed upon my form
I was so cold and damp and scared
and he was flushed and warm
He pressed his feverish lips to mine
I could not make him stop
He drained me of my very self
I gave him every drop
He made me what I am today
that's why you find me here
A little bottle thrown away
that was once filled with beer.

A L Jex

ARCHAEOLOGY ON THE ISLE OF WIGHT

We well may envy those who gaze
perceptively at ages past,
escaping from our modern maze
to probe the secrets long held fast,
and read in shards of moulded clay
the world and work of Bronze Age man,
whose simple relics there betray
his customs and his daily plan,
and clearly see in crudest guise
that nascent waking of the soul,
the birth of art, where untrained eyes
aspired to reach some far-off goal,
still sought when men their scene review,
revolt, reject - create anew.

T C Hudson

65

ISLE OF WIGHT

Visitors are welcome so come here one and all
So much to see and do with lots to enthral
An island full of mystery maybe a ghost or two
So why not come and join us and take in the view
Come here on a day-pass without a passport note
But you'll have to sail across the water
Unless you can float
We have a lot of scenery with history galore
Albert and Queen Victoria loved this island so
Osborne House is famous
Vineyards one or two
But best of all a holiday to suit
We even have a zoo
Blackgang Chine we are losing the sea is claiming more
But now we have a M&S it's got to be worth more
So if you want to sample an island that's serene
Come along and see us to fulfil that lifetime dream.

J Funnell

SPRING

Warmish breezes, caress dawning chirping birds
Budding trees, abundantly flourish
Daffodils, blossoms, snowdrops assuredly cascade the ground
People stride out more cheerfully
Sing aloud, spring has come!

Rebecca Düsoir

OUR ISLAND SHORE

Here, where the rim of the ocean laps on the shore
and slides back, gleaming;
the pulse of the mind slows, till the swish of the sea
is all there is left,
and the body's rhythm tunes to waters
gliding
as water that washed in the womb
before the crying began.

Here, pressing the restless surge of their voices, they come,
brittle, not listening,
nor looking where sky meets ocean, and the eye sees
only the mind's pictures,
where the ear is lulled, body
refreshed
by the lap of water, before
the crying begins again.

Margaret J Tiddy

A LONG DAY

New life, being born is the start of a day
Elevenses, a teenager bright in every way,
Lunchtime, middle-age wise and weary
Teatime, a pensioner and life you query
Suppertime, memories of long ago
Bedtime, goodnight and a sad cheerio.

M D Talmondt

OLD MOVIE

We sat together and watched an old movie.
Black and white, sharp contrasts, an X-ray's definition.
I saw your face soften with remembrance and I knew
You had seen it all before, long ago,
With a lost love, and you thought of her
And smiled.

Your secret's safe with me.
I watched with you and saw my other self
In a darkened picture house,
fanning an ancient flame,
half-forgotten.

I smiled and you sighed,
and we sat together,
the four of us,
and I remembered
I love you.

Tessa Bailey

UNTITLED

Blue and green are seldom seen
that's what I was taught,
but since my revelation
I've had a different thought,
I gazed across the meadow
to a secluded little copse,
where rabbits run
and birds have fun
around the tall treetops,
but the carpet to complete the scene
was bluebells sporting blue and green.

S Love

OH . . . TO BE SLIM

Oh . . . to be slim
is the trend that's in
that's why you'll find me down the gym
working out to impress him
worked out so much, I've hurt a limb
all this, just to be thin!

Oh . . . to be slim
is the trend that's always in
that's why you'll see me eating salads to be thin
and throwing the chocolate in the bin
'cos chocolate's a *sin*
if you want to be slim!

Oh . . . to be slim
is the fashion trend that's still in
but when chocolate's my only whim
how can I be slim?
Just want to be thin!
Maybe then I'll fit *in!*

D L Brown

HAZY ROOM

I walk into the room, as if in a daze,
It swims and swirls, hidden in a haze.
Then it slowly settles back in place,
And as I turn, I see a face.
I nod, and smile, and say hello,
They then reply, and turn to go.
I don't know them, they don't know me,
But it doesn't matter, don't you see?
If we're friends or not, all are the same,
For everyone here is slightly insane.

I stand by a table, then sink to a chair,
And, head in hands, decide to stay there.
Why am I here? I don't really belong,
But anywhere else seems equally wrong.
I raise my head, fiddle with a straw,
I can't get a grip on my thoughts anymore.
People are packed close, but don't see each other,
They're cutting themselves off from one another.
They also are gazing through that weird haze,
Each equally mad, in their own different ways.

Then *they* arrive, familiar faces abound,
Vaguely known people seem to surround.
They chat, as I sit and play with my fork,
And I hear my voice answer their talk.
Someone turns, and passes me a drink,
What is it? Don't ask, don't wonder, don't think.
Just sip and smile, as I laugh, talk, mime,
Act like I'm having a wonderful time.
In a place full of these - misted and hazed -
The foolish, the hopeless, and the depraved.

Yolanda Muckle

THE SEASONS

Spring, is life's awakening;
the forces of nature, tensing and stretching,
ready for the year's renewal
as every heartbeat breathes more life
into the season,
and the simple urgency of living fills
every living thing.

Summer, is life itself;
see buzz and birdsong,
living lakes and breathing winds,
singing trees in silent groves,
and all creatures are busy just living.

Autumn, the world twitches and dies;
leaves fall, dry and scorched, in
nature's destruction,
plants wither and writhe,
and life is bundled up for another year.

Winter, death's snow-white hand;
smothers and chokes the life from
the earth

leaving an eerie silence.

Ross Ogilvie

REMOTE CONTROL

At home,
with the phone.
Who to call?
No-one at all.
What's on TV?
Nothing for me.
A video perhaps?
A viewing relapse.
What to do?
Nothing new.
What to think?
The missing link!
Think about things,
worries and fears.
The boredom suddenly
just disappears.

Andrea Muchowski

THE LOVE BOAT

A trip on a boat is what the girls need
Jumped on a ferry at Sheerness you see . . .
We all had a cabin, a bunk and a loo
What we would find, nobody knew.

Jackie and Fatmah and Paula and me -
We were dancing away while the ship was at sea . . .
There was vodka and brandy, Pernod and gin,
We were looking for hunks to practice some sin!

Fatmah met John, a hunk of a man
With biceps that rippled away in her hands,
He stood with his pals, standing out in the crowd.
Fat's knees were wobbly, she was ever so proud!
Next it was Paula, what was I to do
She met Gary on her way to loo.
'Hello sweetheart' we heard his loud cry,
'Bin for a wee!' I wanted to die!
A nice-looking boy with a bit of a 'tache,
They were snogging so much she broke out in a rash.

Then Jackie, she met the man of the year
With black curly hair and a succulent rear,
Buying her drinks and making her laugh
Then it was me who followed their path.

I met Tony, wow what a guy
Lovely and tall, but really quite shy
We were wild, it was raining, we went on topdeck
Where I realised my make-up had run down my neck.

The moral of stories like this, you must see
Is for us single girls like you, and like me
Get on a ferry, forget all your troubles
And get up that bar, I'll have a double.

Dawn Taylor

PRESTON DOWNS

On July the 16th 1993
We moved to Weymouth by the sea,
Away from busy, bustling towns
To quiet, peaceful Preston Downs.
Green hills surround our small estate
Sheep baa-ing heard from the garden gate.
We took a walk up on the hill
And found a stunning view-to thrill.
Across the bay, sea shimmering blue
The cliffs sheer, white. Oh, what a view!
Portland - majestic in the sea
Looked proud and rugged to John and me.
Then down below us, we saw reeds
That catered for the wild birds' needs,
The oblong waters of Lodmoor Park
With paths for twitchers, light on dark.
The coastline curved with brown and green
So clear that detail could be seen,
Patchy bracken, swathes of clay,
Shingle beaches, fields of hay.
Alas, we cannot stay too long
We turn to go and hear the song,
Of swallows, twittering all around
Fast-flying, swooping near the ground.

As we walk back past Horselynch plantation
We thought that here, Dorset, would be our salvation,
But here the *Brown Route* will one day cut through,
The *planners* - they surely can't make this come true?
Why spoil this - the beautiful county of ours
And home to so many animals, birds, bees, and flowers.

R M Neary

73

DORSET

Summer, autumn, winter and spring
you'll find plenty to Dorset to make your heart sing,
beautiful, quiet leafy lanes
thatched cottages, with leaded window-panes.
Mellow-stoned manor houses standing so grand
surrounded by acres of wooded parkland,
wonderful churches, lichen-clad and weather-worn -
in their happy Sunday Schools our beliefs were born.

Sparkling streams that gurgle and scatter
as down to the sea they bubble and splatter,
little market towns with their narrow streets
all your wants and needs will politely meet.
Wide, green countryside that stretches for miles
where you stand and gaze, your face wreathed in smiles.
Ruins, tumulus, Roman roads and ancient earthworks
are just some of this county's very own quirks,
this is the beauty of Dorset for you to adore
and wherever you travel you'll come back for more.

Margaret Nicklen

UNTITLED

This pain in my heart is all because of you.
Your coldness makes my eyes feel heavy,
ladened with tears.

I spend days waiting for you to return into my life.
The photograph of you sits and faces me in my sleep
with the steady, calm look of knowing on your face.

I worry about you, for you feel like my responsibility,
but I know that it is your life and I should let go
of this hope that you might have any feelings left for me.

But I know that it's impossible, although I just wish
you would consider my feelings for you.
I need to know of your presence and to feel your body
next to mine.

But nothing ever changes, I want to be part of your life
because you are my reason for living and this empty
pain inside is pulling at my emotions, making me
realise how much I love you.

Emily Kidd

UNTITLED

I know I should love you
but something says no
I know I should like you
but still I don't know
There's something about you
I don't understand
A certain something
in a far away land
Just tell me your secrets
let me know how you feel.
I want to be with you
through life's little wheel
To share all the things
that life throws on us
But we cannot do this
if there is no trust
Please learn how to love me
put your life in my hands
I promise not to hurt you
let's go out and expand
Our lives are together
I just want you to know
So please take a chance
and hey, here we go.
Helen Downes (15)

THE PARTY

I met you at a party.
Someone I once knew and liked.
You asked me, so we danced.

A wobbly, bumpy dance was ours; you,
drunk and apologetic; me, sober
(I'm driving, and as my mother advised,
I've watched my drink isn't spiked).

Either you meant it
and were trying to please,
in a masterly way,

Or wanted me to pine after you
and your ego's masterplan.
I pity this delusion.

I'd wanted romance,
but you wanted fun
and maybe even admiration.

Oh, you misjudge me if you think I want this.
We waste time on the grass-tufts of love
and I am disappointed.

Or maybe I misjudge myself
as I enjoyed your attentions.
Yet, despite my wishes

I know it shouldn't work.
It is drunken pointlessness
to continue believing.

And so I find that my fear
of falling in love too close
in a doomed relationship
has led me to hate you.

Abi Mansley

TO MY SWEETHEART - LOVE IS THE THING

Every time I think of you, my heart beats so fast
I'm thinking of the future now, not the long lost past,
Since you came into my life, I'm full of the joys of spring
I wonder what you've done to me, *love is the thing.*

When I sit just thinking, I think of days gone by
And every day is better, without even having to try,
I take each day as it comes and I feel that I could sing
I don't know what you've done to me, *Love is the thing.*

You take my hand and walk with me along the busy street
And when we walk into a park together we take a seat,
When you look into my eyes, you make my heart go zing!
I've no idea what you've done to me, but *love is the thing.*

I'll end this poem by saying 'Will you marry me?'
Please give me an answer, don't let me wait and see.,
And on that special day I'll give you a wedding ring
Now I know what you've done to me *love is the thing.*

Alan Robertson

SUMMER JOY

Oh the beauty of the country
When the sun shines down, it seems
All the joy of summer bounty
Is in reality, not dreams.

The birds sing in the woodland,
The grass is green, serene,
And walking through we understand
What happiness has been.

But now the mist's upon the land
And dark and damp, grey days,
Covering the land we'd planned
For happiness to raise.

So what has happened to our world?
Where did love and beauty go?
The ecstasy of love unfurled,
The joy we all should know.

We pray the sun will shine again
That the earth be cleaned and pure
So that once again goodness will reign
And love fore'er endure.

I long to be in the countryside
With the air so fresh and clean,
And above all have a horse to ride
Through myriad fields of green!

Gilda Libbish

DANCING DREAMS

I look in the mirror before walking out the door
And think of all the times I've been here before.
Why do you do this, a voice says to me?
I want to have fun, is that so impossible to see?
I look back at the mirror with a scowl on my face
I feel anxious inside and long to dance in that place.
I am happy when I'm there, so good I do feel
When I'm in my own world where my dreams are so real.
I dance all night long, no feelings I hide
The beat of the music, with friends by my side.
But the night has to end
Just like before,
But the dream is still alive
And I know there are plenty more.

Tamzin Hardy

WINTER

Summer's gown, torn and tattered,
Fragments held, then careless cast,
The odd remaining scraps of colour,
Sad reminders of days long past.

Trees now bare and solitary,
Stand erect, with arms held high,
As if in silent plea for mercy,
Are mocked by slate-grey, angry sky,

Cold brown earth with life encrusted,
But hidden deep, like miser's store,
While all around a blanket stillness,
And wind that whispers, wait once more.

Elizabeth Whitehead

ISLE OF PURBECK

The Purbeck Hills' calm curves suggest
A lady in repose:
Corfe Castle is her tired head,
Old Harry Rocks her toes.

She sees the Satyrs lie and romp
And with half-open eye,
She watches some dune denizen,
Unfed, collapse and die.

He'd clambered up and tottered down
The dunes where rushes grew:
Her body was what circumscribed
The futile world he knew.

Her body, slim, symmetrical,
Gives all protection where
The Naiads and the smooth snakes rest
Beyond the curse of care.

While resting on her bed of bog,
She lets crude men despoil
Her prehistoric reservoirs
In their mad thrust for oil.

Miss Purbeck's lank naiveté
Has power and instils
An urge to know the fate that lurks
Behind recumbent hills.

E J Williams

UNDER THE BLOOD-RED CLOUDS OF VAZON

The sea and the sand are in love you said
And we watched as they reached out
Gingerly, daring to touch
Ever so gently
Under skies iced and spiteful,
In the space before evening.
Trickles of water, like mucus,
Traced lines on the skin of the sand
And massaged, caressed the furrows
As smooth as darkness.
The sand, held in its grip,
Groaned in its pleasure.

Later, as we sat in the warmth
Of the kitchen's embrace
I thought of them down on the beach
Rolling over and over
In an ecstasy of salt,
Whilst overhead
The clouds bled.

M Dickinson

WALKS UPON KINGSCLERE DOWNS

Ancient rolling hills always richly green
in my heart instills fond memories when seen.
Eager feet so anxious to tread every lonely, winding track
eyes feasting upon Hampshire beauty, whenever glancing back.
Distant views so often shrouded in a soft, misty haze
even on summer evenings, beneath the setting sun's rays.

Sounds of sheep bleating fills the evening air
birdcalls fast and fleeting, echo everywhere.
Golden fields of hay glow amongst fields of meadow grass
waiting to be gathered in, before the long summer days pass.
Many wildflowers grow, hidden well from human view
amongst tall-bladed grass, their colours peeping through.

Bright-red dancing poppy, golden buttercup
offer sweet nectar for searching bees to sup.
White-headed daisies and clovers, pink and white
fill the air with perfumes, both by day and night.
Sometimes the sound of noisy, passing traffic floats above the hill
reminding each happy rambler, for the Downs, time at least
                                                    stands still.

M M Davey

THE TENNYSON DOWNS, FRESHWATER, ISLE OF WIGHT

It's a beautiful walk down to Freshwater Bay
and then, after sitting a while
to look at the large white sea-horses at play
as they scamper and scurry and soak you with spray
take the lane up to Watcombe, and over the stile.

You'll find yourself then on a wide stretch of land
with a good sturdy climb to the fore;
you leave far behind you the Bay with its sand
and, as you go climbing, with breezes you're fanned
from the sea, as it beats on the shore.

Your goal reached at last, and the cross there you see
standing proudly on top of the hill
and it's there on that spot that great peace comes to me -
the air is just glorious, my spirit is free -
and the world all around lies so still.

A great panorama of beauty is there
stretching widely for mile upon mile
Hurst Castle lighthouse and Yarmouth seem near
(in days now long past you'd see Alum Bay pier) -
what a glorious and grand little isle.

Totland and Colwell lie just 'round the bend
in peaceful tranquillity.
You welcome each landmark you see as a friend
for the many sweet beauties, they just seem to blend
in a vale of humility.

Humility that this loveliness, rare
should be ours to enjoy when we will.
No wonder Lord Tennyson loved to sit there
and on paper, inscribe thoughts for others to share -
thoughts that live in our memory still.

Joyce Newlin

DAWN

Early morning in a frost-bound field
The ice is crunching under my feet,
White and crisp the frozen grass
The earth is still, so cold, asleep.

The blood-red dawn stains the sky
Pushing out from the womb of night,
The flowing flesh of another day
Yawning its way into the light.

The crimson life-tide ripples out
And tops the silent, sentinel trees,
Giving substance to their naked limbs
Adding colour to their shaking leaves.

The moment of silent awe is now
Before the sun blinds the searching eye,
My heart is bursting in sympathy with
The life that is surging through the sky.

P D Tas

COASTAL EROSION

The coastal cliffs of sand and clay
Relentlessly rained on day after day,
Sodden and seeping
Wet and weeping,
Like a woman in waiting
The waters break,
But happy outcome - no.
The birth of these cliffs was decades ago.
Now just destruction as they slide their way
To the shore below.
Here waterfalls, there rivulets,
Taking the slurry, slipping and sliding,
In colourful streams of white, green and brown,
Down, down, down,
Washed by the sea on the shore at high tide,
The loss of the land which caused such emotion
Another chapter in coastal erosion.

Patricia Allen

SAINT CATHERINE'S HILL (TWYFORD DOWN)

Half-way up, and the hilltop came in sight . . .
Trees in a ring locked, and split up the light.
I turned to see where I'd come from -
A bell rang faint, from Christendom
I lay me down in an old kingdom
Lay me down at its gate.

Two thousand years to the brave bright song of the lark . . .
Rampart high . . . and footfalls out in the dark.
The lookouts tense at undertones
The hissing breezes sift their bones

A scream

And blindly cracking stones
Hit the rush too late.

Fire in the ditch - split blocks clatter apart
Fire in the huts - a torch, a torch in the heart
Nowhere to turn, nowhere to run
Just hate and kill to the smoking sun
All will
Die
When the dogs have won

Pain and axe

Await.

Round broken walls, the weasel seeks out prey
Hawk on the breeze floats - and falls back away.
No sound now from the slopes below,
How smooth the ribbon rivers flow

Go now

As the shadows grow
Deep dark be slow . . .

Night wait.

Alan Bolesworth

DORSET

A delightful triangle so unique
With pretty villages quaint and neat
Where farming is the way of life
For father, son and sometimes wife
Heathlands full of heather hue
Hide deer and fox and badger too
Magnificent views from hilltops high
Where buzzards soar and skylarks fly
And in the patchwork fields below
Rippling grass comes fit to mow
Snoozing cows are fat and full
Young heifers harass worn-out bull
Sheep content lay in the sun
Lambs run riot having fun
Over hill a sea so blue
Beaches of sand and pebble too
Ochre cliffs reach for the sky
Seabirds flock and screech and cry
Fishing boats leave quiet quay
To an unknown destiny
Then people arrive by the score
It's holiday time down here once more
Caravans invade our place
There's others in the human race
Traffic queues on every road
Angers all young and old
Bed and breakfast signs appear
Soon *full up* words are clear
But for certain we can say
There ain't no motorways down our way.

Margaret Weller

I LOVE DORSET

As the winds blow
you should know
the beauty of Dorset

The seas crash
splash by splash
the birds hover
up and down

It's nice to get away
to watch the sea
come to me
wave by wave

Water runs 'round and 'round
I listen to the flow
taking over the lands
the rivers run like hands

The smell of the flowers blooming
the cottages with the colours bright
the colours of the countryside
what a beautiful sight

The grass grows
as time goes by
it makes the countryside unique
the hi-tec world's too much for me
that's why I love Dorset.

Sarah Bosanquet

DORSET

Down in deepest Dorset dear
Right where the turnips grow
The farmers reap and sow
Cows and sheep
They do moo and bleat

Down in deepest Dorset dear
Barn owls' eyes are open wide
Blinking and winking cosily inside
Cockerels crowing in the morning
People getting up and yawning

Down in deepest Dorset dear
In the pubs people are singing
On Sundays church bells are ringing
Farmers are gathering in the corn
Birds sing at crack of dawn
Down in deepest Dorset dear.

Ann Sylvia Franks

HOLIDAY TIME

I might go camping for a week
A friend of mine has lent
Something in a canvas bag
That's supposed to be a tent

There were no instructions with it
It just looked one big mess
As to where the poles go
I'll just have to guess

I struggled for an hour or two
That was enough for me
I really lost my patience
So I went and made some tea

I picked up the daily paper
And printed on page three
Holidays for sixty quid
That will do for me

There were lovely little caravans
Or chalets I could pick
The thought of putting that tent up
Made me feel quite sick

I quickly made my mind up
A chalet I will rent
I'll holiday in luxury
Not crawl into a tent

I know my friend will laugh at me
She'll say it's guts I lack
But I'll come up with the lame excuse
I've gone and hurt my back.

Sheila Rowley

DAN!

I don't know how
to say or put this,
when you're around
my mind stays blank,
the tears I cry
are in self-pity,
for love I know that won't find.

I know for sure you have a heart
but no-one yet has touched the key,
drifting thoughts and contemplating
reminds me who I want to be.

Emma-Louise Oswin

A TASTE OF WIMBORNE

Minster standing proud and tall
Life-sized soldier on the wall
Strikes his bells for all to hear
The time goes quickly when you're near
People watching on the green
Don't their faces look serene
Corrmarket holding classes there
For adults writing works so rare
Antiques fair, what fun to find
A bargain of a different kind
Many shops to browse around
Library too - don't make a sound
Banks galore - should there be more
Maybe ten, maybe a score?
Restaurants selling delicious fare
Hurry soon to see what's there
Sample apple cake and cream
Which melts in your mouth just like a dream

Beryl O'Brien

THE PARK

I am sitting on a damp park swing,
A man is pledging undying love with a ring,
With leaves and acorns falling on my head
And children emerging dirty from the flowerbed.

As I make my way down to the pond edge,
I see a pink coat fly over the hedge
And a little girl with her teddy Ed,
With two ducks attacking each other's head.

Two children jumping into a puddle,
Getting their mother into a muddle,
Ducks being thrown bread from loving hands
And children making castles in the sand.

This is a typical autumn haze,
That has lots of people in a daze,
A man in disappointment of being turned down
And conkers falling from trees like jewels from a crown.

As everything goes cold and dark,
I leave this damp and dismal park,
Well . . . for today at least!

Gail Lugget

IT'S A GOOD JOB . . .

I get out of dread
Brush my seeth
Climb down the worry
To the hope beneath.
I put on my gloat,
And look in the sinner,
Open the bore
And notice the glimmer.
Nothing to do,
Nothing at all,
Cry in my coffee
Stare at the wall.
Jobless is hopeless,
Hopeless too roomy,
I tie up my mirth
And find myself gloomy.
Happy is hopeful
Hopeful is ugly
I find myself
Darker than lovely.

Lisa Smedley

DORSET THOUGHTS

I walk with God,
Where quiet flows the Frome,
Where minnows dart,
And kingfishers call home
The reeded banks;
And wing with jewelled gleam
Of lapis lazuli,
Where every stream
Tinkles soft cadences;
Lush meadows lie
All opulent,
Beneath a summer sky:
Bee murmurings,
And browsing cattle nod;
Here, in sweet solitude,
I walk with God.

I walk with God,
Where climbs the wooded height,
Where timid deer
Venture, half-poised for flight;
And upland paths
Bedecked with hedgerows green,
Plunge down,
To hidden valleys half-unseen,
And a lone kestrel
Hovers on the wing,
Seeking his prey,
Whilst swelling blackbirds sing;
Where orchids bloom
In secret glades untrod,
Here, with a thankful heart,
I walk with God.

Doris J Walker

POETIC HIGH

Are you a person
Who says poetry is a bore?
Have you thought about this?
Are you really sure?

For putting pen to paper
Brings a wondrous sense to me
Like flying in an air-balloon
Or paddling by the sea

Sometimes I'll sit for hours
Perfecting every line
At others I'll just scribble
Until my pen runs dry

But how I write my poetry
Or what I write about
Really does not matter
It just lets my feelings out

For when I write these words down
I'm unsure what will come out
But an enormous weight is lifted
Of that I have no doubt!

Allyson Ward

18-PLUS

Oh what fun we have,
every Thursday is such a laugh,
quizzes and games to play,
18-plus is here to stay.

We meet up in a local bar,
everyone comes from near and far,
all the time we get new faces,
they all come from different places.

No nastiness amongst the crowd,
some are quiet, some are loud,
some are young, some are old,
some see adverts, some are told.

When you go to a meeting too,
happy people all the night through,

The weekends are normally fun,
discos and sports in the sun,
meeting new people in every place,
at the next even you'll remember that face.

Oh I've never had so much fun,
that's why 18-plus is for everyone.

Linzi Taylor

CONTENT

Now I'm someone of habit,
I rise at seven and feed my rabbit,
Breakfast, wash and dress,
Then make orderly any mess,
So I go on from day to day,
I know that you would say,
This certainly seems bleak,
But at the end of the week,
To keep life sweet,
I give myself a little treat,
And I trot down the road,
As I go into a relaxing mode,
And return, money well-spent,
I sit back and enjoy,
A fine wine from the continent.

I Coates

LEAVING

Let me kiss your tender lips
run fingers through your hair,
let me feed upon your passion
as fiercely as I dare.
Let me touch my tongue to yours
feel its electric spark,
let me tell you physically
how deep you've left your mark.
Let me feel your skin so soft
you in turn feel mine,
let me know just once more
how making love can be so fine.
Let me take you by the hand
stroll through endless miles,
let me see your happiness
through your eyes within your smiles.
Let me fold you in my arms
protect and hold you near,
let me remember your beauty
when you're no longer here.

Paula Edwards

CANVASSED TEMPLES

In tents
Lovers of outdoors
Show respect
By worshipping
The world from canvassed temples
Underneath a dome where
Diamonds are exhibited upon black velvet.

Soman Balan

EXCITING HOBBIES

I want exciting hobbies
that will make my friends all gasp.
But daring, scary hobbies
I can never fully grasp.

I tried my hand at bungee jumping
leaping from a cliff.
My Mum had starched the bungee rope
and made it really stiff.

I tried to catch a bus that day
but couldn't quite get on.
The problem with the rope I had
was forty-nine feet long.

So then I tried to hang-glide
I bought all the trendy gear.
But when I launched into the air
I couldn't really steer.

I flew and flew then flew some more
I kept on going higher.
The gear's all in my garage now
I still can't find a buyer.

Morris dancing, fencing, rowing
I have tried the lot.
I even tried clay pigeons once
but kept on getting shot.

I do not understand the reason
why my hobbies fail.
But with all the stock I've got
I'll hold a garage sale.

Spencer Boston

THE JOYS OF CAMPING

Our legs begin to buckle and we sag against the strain
Of carting 'round backpacks in the cold and dismal rain
But finally we drop the tent and find the perfect spot
To have a happy weekend, full of romance? . . . I think not.

My mind had conjured images of candles, wine and song
Naughty nibbles, massages and smooching all night long
But sadly disillusioned, I battle through the storm
And try to make that tent of ours begin to look like home.

The rain is lashing in my face, it dribbles down my nose
Then icy winds start blowing, and soon the drops have froze
Tiny little icicles forming on my skin
Sticking to my nostrils and my eyelashes and chin.

I steal a look across the frame, to see how he is faring
And instead of putting up the tent I find that he is staring
At two gorgeous little dolly birds, all make-up, heels and pouts
So I grab him by the collar and give him such a clout.

The girls begin to giggle as he hurries back to work
I hurt his fragile ego when I made him look a berk
But finally it's assembled and into it we do crawl
And then I see it looming, a great big sodden hole.

All I need is a swimsuit and a yellow rubber duck
For the tent is filled with water, I don't believe my luck
Gingerly I lean across to try and mend the rip
A gentle shove off him, and into the tent I trip.

Sprawled out in the water, like a big fat stranded whale
Who needs a camping holiday, stuck up in the Dales?
I march off in disgust, he can stay there on his own
For I'm going somewhere cosy, to the warmth that I call home.

Louise Saul

LIFE

Life is not always so thrilling,
Sometimes I feel lonely and sad,
But, when looking around I see others,
And realise my life's not so bad.

Some people are homeless and starving,
Others are jobless and broke,
Some have life-threatening diseases,
My problems must seem like a joke.

Problems like mine seem like nothing,
But lots of things cause me stress,
Overworking, health problems, depression,
It makes everything seem such a mess.

Most of the time I'm so happy,
But sometimes it's just an act,
I don't want to cause other people worry,
They have problems of their own - it's a fact.

When feeling sorry for myself I just think,
Of all the things in my life that are good,
My family are worth more than words can say,
Problems - they've always understood.

No-one knows how long we'll all live,
Everyone has to die,
But for now I'll count myself lucky,
I'm just thankful to be alive.

Marie Fidell

THE SINGLE LIFE

Sitting in front of the mirror drying my hair,
Does it matter what I look like, will anyone care?
I sometimes think if I had a bag on my head,
Someone would still try and get me into bed.

I take my time with my make-up and clothes,
Making sure I look right from my head to my toes.
As soon as I'm outside my hair is a mess,
Why I bother is anyone's guess.

My friend is single too and feeling a little down,
So tonight we're going out to hit the town.
Two girls together painting the town red,
Hungry for men like we've never been fed.

We walk into the bar and I have a quick glance,
Maybe I'll bump into *Mr Right,* just by chance.
He's definitely not here, I'm kidding myself,
It's *Mr Not So Right,* or stay on the shelf.

I haven't decided yet which I like best,
So in the meantime i'll keep on with my quest.
Tonight's a night we're going to have some fun,
Well, it's that or get depressed and become a nun.

We have a few drinks and get a bit happy,
We're getting stared at by a boy, complete with nappy.
Then it's the turn of the dirty old man,
Complete with hairpiece and tub of fake tan.

I always seem to attract the ones that are odd,
Thinking they're a gift to women sent by God.
I'll never find *the man* while I'm in this pub,
Am I desperate enough to join a singles club?

M Donnalley

LIVING ALONE AND UNEMPLOYED

I'm happy and I'm surrounded by friends,
All laughing, telling jokes and having fun,
Then I wake up and my dream just ends,
And there's no-one here, I'm the only one.

As I lay in my bed staring at the ceiling,
I try and find reason for starting today,
And all I end up with is the same old feeling,
That my loneliness is with me to stay.

When I do finally rise, I make some tea,
And dress and wash and make up my face,
And when I'm all ready, I watch TV,
Where my substitute friends are all in place.

And maybe at three, I'll pick up the 'phone,
And call someone, just for a voice to hear,
And for a few minutes, I don't feel alone,
With a piece of plastic up against my ear.

As the evening draws in, I start to plan,
I change my clothes and wash my hair,
Then I go into town and meet the gang,
And listen to stories they want to share.

At eleven, I drink up and say my goodbyes,
By the time I get home, I'm wrapped in sorrow,
So I put on some music and close my eyes,
In a desperate attempt to delay tomorrow.

Janis Bartlett

THE END

The looks from strangers are making me ill,
My pale face is noticed still,
But why must I hide, not open my door
Or when I go out, keep my face to the floor?
It's not up to me how people react,
When they see me so drawn and all dressed in black.
When I look in the mirror all that I see
Is the sad lonely girl who used to be me.
Whatever happened to the bright rosy cheeks,
Or the smile that hasn't been seen in weeks?
I lie on my bed with my eyes to the sky
And all I ever ask is the question, Why?
My life's a mess and nobody cares,
My problems so many, I just need to share.
But who wants to listen to a person like me?
I should just end it here and throw away the key.
Nobody knows of the hurt that I feel
I don't even know myself if it's real.
I long to smile and show that I care
But if I do who's going to be there?
No-one listens or understands
My friends so many I could count on one hand.
I want it to end, and the pain to leave,
The torment I bear I have to perceive.
There's nobody out there, there's nowhere to hide
So the hurt that I feel must stay inside.
Would anyone worry if I wasn't here,
Would they notice, even shed a tear?
Nobody ever asks me why?
Now the pain has all gone, and it's too late to cry.

Kelly Joseph (16)

DORSET

Stand tall my friend, on top the Ridgeway brow,
Fill there your lungs with salted air.
Facing north sees chalk, soil and sow,
Seagulls squawking, swoop and follow yonder plough.
If ever a time to look back, 'twere now!

The sea so blue, harnessed by undulating land
Arcing round - cliff, pebble to golden sand
Like paint unloaded from artist's brush,
Swept onto canvas in a tender rush.
If ears could focus like one's eyes,
You would hear the Punch and Judy cries out loud.
Take Hardy's Wessex far from this madding crowd.

Oh Dorset lush with differing green,
Likened to a quilt layed of fair maiden's hand.
No levelling of ground or need there to prepare.
This patchwork quilt was formed by God,
With thought and loving care.

Fields of blue linseed next to bright yellow rape,
Moving gently onwards - golden, brown to vivid greens.
No stitches here to see:
God used hedgerows for his seams.

Each field has its own personal gate,
Rusted red by rain and time,
Secure as be needed with old bailing twine.

Yet, beauty brings people and people bring cars
And with them come 20th century scars,
Like signs saying:
Do not leave valuables in cars.

Malcolm Harris

HOLIDAY ISLE

When you plan a holiday
I wonder where you go
To the sunny French Riviera
Or Switzerland with snow?

Take a trip to the Isle of Wight
And see its beauty rare,
Its seaside towns and villages
And views beyond compare.

There are lovely sandy beaches
Where children safely play,
At Blackgang there's a theme park
You'll want to stay all day.

In the centre of the island
Where all the coaches stop
Is Godshill, with thatched cottages
And church on the hilltop.

On the western tip is Freshwater
With a climb up Tennyson Down,
Alum Bay with coloured sands
Yarmouth - a harbour town.

There are animals in plenty
Some of them quite rare,
There is no need to hurry
Take time to stop and stare.

As you sail across the Solent
On your homeward way,
With memories of the island
You'll wish that you could stay.

P M Attrill

NO RETURN

I know the trails that call aloud,
and paths that lie in summer sun,
where neck-high parsleys reek so sweet,
sunk deep in drowsy insect hum.

Just climb the tumbling drystone wall
and dye your boots in buttercup.
Then tread the sea-pink carpeting
down to the shimmering seal pup.

Go stumbling down the falling slope
of rolling hill, there see the grass
move in a silver drifting wave
as every blade bows down while breezes pass.

See camouflaging sun and shade
designs along the village street,
there all our childhood lovers walked,
and all our days and hours were sweet.

Oh island home, home of my youth,
why haunt me with your sun and skies?
You know the chains that tie my life
are stronger than your urgent cries.

Phil Wills

WALKING HOME

The pavement moves uneasily beneath the feet
Faster
Faster
A stumbling confrontation as
The knife cuts the screams in two
Trauma
Distress
Hand over mouth
Thumb compressing trachea
Awareness terrorised by the calculation
Frenetic fumbling

Penetration

Tension transferred from one to another
Leaving the scene
Balaclava intact
Demented

Only devastation persists
Abandoned
Frigid
Bleeding and trembling
A silent oblivious hulk remains

Paul Tarpey

MAYTIME

In her pretty bonnet of blossoms
May dances with the breeze
But all too soon the flowers fade
And petals their freedom will seize.

Like confetti they sprinkle the gardens
And through open windows they peep
Then gleefully chase along roadways
Into all nooks and crannies they creep.

Some will weave beautiful carpets
In colours of pink, red and white
To spread on the ground before us
A wondrous gift of delight.

To treasure, and remind us
Precious moments we must seize
And keep in memory till May returns
To prettily dance with the breeze.

Amelia Canning

ISLE WIGHT AND SEA

Waiting at home on the clifftop
And gazing towards the ocean,
Such overwhelming beauty
Fills my soul with emotion.

The sunshine bright on the water,
The white whispy clouds floating high,
The seagulls, wheeling and circling
Across the blue unthreatening sky.

My eyes follow the steamers
On their daily trips to France;
Till they dip beneath the horizon
In a shimmering mystical dance;

While on the edge of the cliff
From warren to warren it passes,
A stoat hunting for rabbits
Can be glimpsed behind the grasses.

Then I scan the crests of the waves.
Hither and thither I seek
The silvery back of a sea bass
Or a tern with a smelt in its beak;

And on some lucky occasions
A seal bobs up from below;
Sniffs the air for a moment
And is gone where seals must go;

Whilst I relaxed and tranquil
Am happy as happy could be,
Domiciled here on the island
Above the cerulean sea.

Edward Lyon

NOSTALGIA BAH HUMBUG

Nostalgia is the art of believing
That the good old days really did exist
But I believe nostalgia is a disease
And the good old days are really a myth

For example with all honesty
How many Sudanese will look back
With a warm heart's glow at the
Famine that ravages their land?
Sitting by a campfire swapping
Anecdotes of the time they had
Distended stomachs and starved
To death lying on the sand
And what about the one where
The refugee camp was attacked
By troops with grenade and guns?
With all honesty can you tell me
That you would cite that as a
Memory that was fun?

Nostalgia is the art of believing
In the stiff upper lip and camaraderie
But what about rationing, poor sanitation
Nostalgia is an anagram of lost again you see

What about the people of
Northern Ireland will they remember
Fondly over 20 years of violence?
Yes, but! There's Thunderbirds and
Stingray and Captain Scarlet - however
In effect this is only nonsense
Nostalgia is fine and memories
Are good but don't make the memory
Your sacred cow
Because if you do you'll miss so much
Of the beauty of living in the here and now . . .

Francis McFaul

WAR (UTOPIA)

Finding comfort from where you came,
nothing will ever be the same,
no-one knows you or even cares,
standing before you with glaring stares.
Unfamiliar feelings appear to go wild,
forgotten how it was to be a child,
leave it behind to try another way,
try not to listen to what they say.
Who sings to you on stormy nights,
makes you believe that this is right?
You should escape away from this dark,
see the bright sunlight,
shining from the top,
sparkling tenderly, love is mine,
seeing is knowing, feeling is believing,
understanding for the first time that
deceit is a lie, lying is deceiving,
counting the moves, worshipping each one,
hold onto each day as it comes.
The strength of the warmth,
the strength of the sun,
peace comes naturally,
holding back the guns.

Eve Ashwell

POLLUTION

Pollution, pollution, pollution,
We hear about it, we see it,
Are we bothered, do we care?

The rain which gave life
Is now the acid rain of strife,
It's killing the animals, birds, fish,
It has no bounds, the fields and the forests
Are razed to the ground.

The lands lay barren, yet there is more than this,
The ozone is depleted, we even sunbathe at risk.

Our children are born into a world they don't understand,
Do we as adults, or is it we don't give a damn?

What should we do to right the wrongs?
Send letter, campaign, protest, sing songs,
Yet should we need to do these things?
For if the people of the world don't change, no-one will win.

It's up to one and all,
There is a lot of work, the order is told,
But let's start before it's too late,
So that our children may then wake
To a fresh new world of understanding, hope and love.

M Smith

I HAVE A GOLDEN HEART

I have a golden heart my dear,
that promised never to part my dear,
now tell me if my love you'll share,
or have you lost that feel to care?

Maybe at the right time somewhere,
you will give to me all my dear,
but when I'm down and find things hard to bare,
do you promise to be there?

Bittersweet is what I am,
bitter for the weak,
but sweeter for the strong,
my kind of love you can endure for long,
but am as bitter as gall,
if you are found in the wrong.

Jennifer Gayle

THE ENVIRONMENT

The pollution around us
Is certainly destroying us,
So come now, read on with us,

Acid rain destroys the crops,
And weakens all the birds of prey,
So now we're hurting all the flock,
The birds are going away,

The rainforests are being destroyed,
By hungry mechanical monsters,
All the animals there are annoyed,
We're driving them out of their homes,

The ozone layer is being destroyed,
By those terrible CFC's,
The ice will melt, terrifying floods will come,
This done by you and me,

Please help the animals of our world,
By being good and kind,
Please stop pollution, please stop right now,
Or you will kill mankind.

Jenny Smith

BEAUTY

I saw her face so beautiful
and loved her from the start
Her high cheekbones and rosebud lips
a truly work of art

I saw her in my dreams at night
with all her lovely charms
And I would love to hold her
in my eager loving arms

So I resolved to buy her
and placed her in the car
No need now to long for her
or view her from afar

I put her on my bedroom wall
in a golden gilded frame
She is the fairest of them all
and Beauty is her name.

John R Calvert

SALISBURY CATHEDRAL SPIRE

A tall grey finger pointing
upwards to the sky,
built by men of vision
in the days gone by.

A tall grey finger pointing
into the black of night,
brilliantly illuminated
by the clear floodlight.

A tall grey finger vanishing
into the cold grey mist;
clouds that slowly drift aside
with hint of sunshine kissed.

A tall grey finger pointing
towards the golden sun,
which fades into a soft warm glow
when the day is done.

The tall grey finger pointing
shows each of us the way,
through the darkness, mist and clouds
into the glorious day.

Olive Soutar

THINK OF ME

Think of me when you are playing
Whether it's a new or old toy
Just a thought
Think of me when your pastime brings noise and joy
Just a thought
Think of me when at school
Remember what I showed you
Remember what I taught
Think of me when you're feeling unwell
Just a thought
When you cannot explain where the hurt is
Or you have a secret and cannot tell
Think of me
Just a thought.

M Burridge

SOUTHERN DESTRUCTION

The sun glistened between marching waves,
gulls screamed above.
The horizon broke. Sail boats like buoys, came to view, and faded.
White horses strode up seaweed-laden beaches, jostled amongst
the breaks.
Cars disappeared into backroads. Buildings stood, old, derelict,
and wind-blown trees swayed to the nearing storm.
The sea seemed grey, gulls dirty brown.
It came,
thrashing sea to shore, whipping tree from root,
encasing the sky with dark, heaving clouds.
The sea rose,
sail boats like buoys flung skywards,
then died -
broken limb strewn pathways, beaten coast, southern destruction.

Claire Rosenberg

NEWTOWN CREEK

Within the diamond lies the gleam,
Where sea lakes join to ebb and stream;
Earthly glimpse of Heaven's features;
Paradise for all God's creatures.

Unspoiled, so far - but only just;
In jeopardy - past greeds, and lust;
Marauding Frenchmen sent to pillage,
Unwittingly bestowed an ancient village.

Streets *gold,* and *silver,* by-and-by,
The old town hall stands high-and-dry.
Hark! The ghostly piper in the dark,
Did no-one's children reach the *Ark?*

Town and commerce thus averted;
Rural status re-asserted.
Six centuries on, save by thwarted access,
Could heaven abide man's nuclear abscess?

Past Clamerkin, Spur, Causeway, and Corf,
To Western Haven, and Shalfleet's wharf.
Rich silted wetlands, bill-probed and spooned;
Twice-daily banquets - oh gracious moon!

See heron, and curlew, 'pipers, and 'shanks;
Wigeon and brents graze wintry banks;
Orange-billed 'catchers patrolling wet rocks,
Gorging on oysters from Clamerkin's stocks!

The creek is a haven for lovers of boats;
Real sailors - boating - no brass-buttoned coats;
It's no place for *yotties* - hi-tech boats from Cowes;
It's sloops, gaffs, and cutters - and a-huggin' of Scows.

Hail deepest Solent! Most blessed of moats;
Invaders contained by their ferries and boats;
No barrage, no bridge, no multiple spanners.
God! Spare all this beauty from vandals and planners.
L V Hall

KALEIDOSCOPE

Come down to lovely Dorset, where
You'll find kind folk and clean fresh air
Where days are long but time just flies
And dazzling colours still surprise

See Lulworth Skippers, Chalkhill Blues
Fritillaries of many hues
The yellow ragwort on display
And popping gorse in bright array

From Aldheim's Head to Portland Bill
The turquoise sea is never still
And multicoloured ducks compete
With whitened swans safe in the Fleet

Such pretty watercourses flow
Where umber reed-mace solemn grow
And there below the sparkling stream
Viridian watercresses gleam

There's copper beech and silver birch
And bluebell woods beyond the church
Where poplar black and poplar white
With lime and chestnut bring delight

There's shades and tones and dyes and tints
Of orange, green, maroon and pink
There's amber, ochre, bronze and brown
From Golden Cap to Ballard Down

Here *is* the place to stand and stare
Try out some tempting country fare
So, how about a nice cream tea
And Dorset folk for company?

C C Sealy

UNTITLED

One should be a poet or poetess
to write of Counties in the South-West.

Dorset
Lovely miles of Chesil beach
Holiday is in the mind
Refreshed body, walk relaxed
Eyes move towards the sea
Forget hassle, hurried man
Take Dorset coastal land
Our way of feeling new life and limb.

Devon
Villages with view of moors
Miles of slower travel
It is there to find
Hushed beauty of Eggesford fishing rights
Never-ending ground to explore
Time to stand or sit, just stare
Shape of forest, high green hills
Wonderful Devon jewel.

Cornwall
As some call the Rugged Rock
Tamar Bridge across
Known as a different world!
Won't get time to do it *all*
Deep-sea fishing, catch that whale
East and West of Looe
Even smell of fish is great
On the quayside, busy lot!
The hardest thing is about-turn, take
our leave, make room for others.

E K Wakeford

BEAUTY OF DORSET

Did you see Dorset in your dreams -
rolling hills and valleys serene?
Scent of wild roses in the spring,
the joy to the bird, it makes him sing.
Footpaths and byways away from the highways,
outstanding beauty to walk along to breathe the air.
God gave this for us to share the
hills, the valleys, the sky, the sea.
Surely you've seen Dorset in your dreams,
blue sky, blue sea meets coast so green.
Wild birds and wild flowers on hills and valleys,
ditches and dykes by marsh and ponds,
rivers and streams by sand and rock.
Such beauty everywhere just waiting to be seen.

Reg Cooper

FRESHWATER

This quiet village set in the West Wight
With its well-kept gardens filled with flowers bright
The fishing boats lie anchored clustered in the bay
The seagulls call to welcome in this fresh new day.

And as the dawn breaks over the vast shimmering sea
The rugged cliffs stand clearly out against the sky
On wings of song a lark soars high as if set free
White clouds across the blue expanse pass slowly by.

The thatched church of St Agnes full of olde worlde charm
For many a wary traveller it is a soothing balm
Still people come to gather there and give God praise
The old and young united their joyful voices raise.

The shops in this small village provide for all we need
The dress shops, grocers, bakers the hungry mouths to feed
Health clinic, dentist, printers, schools and the football field
The rolling farmland 'round us its rich abundance yield.

The river Yar flows gently onward to the sea
And south-east across the causeway All Saints stands solidly
As back in Norman times this fine stone church was built
All down through the ages symbol of stability.

So now as evening shadows fall and sun is set
A bright star shines from the clear summer sky
We can thank God for He the day has blessed
Contented here we live until we are called on high.

Helen Mew

MY WIGHT ISLAND

To walk along the beaches,
strolling hand in hand.
Each wave just gently lapping,
with bare feet in the sand.

Above you see green pastures,
and blue skies all around.
Also sheep are grazing,
on the rich and sodden land.

An island full of beauty,
wherever you may look.
Rich in beautiful colours,
that you would never find in a book.

There's rolling hills and countryside,
and historic places you can see.
Queen Victoria lived here,
a place so quaint but free.

Lesley Everson

116

THE HAND OF ROY
This temple took more than three days to rebuild

From cathedral air (Notre Damp)
To drier vent
And all floors in between,
The uprise of damp
Revolt of rot
The hand of Roi
Or Roy is seen.

From two brass screws
To the fourth cot leg
And all walls in between,
The tops of tiles
The skirt of boards
The hand of Roi
Or Roy is seen.

Time is skips and sugar lumps.
(Two for Gary none for Roy)
Then again the wailing calls
Of loosely plastered walls
Beg healing from the hand of Roy.

Martin Kiszko

GOWER COAST

Gleaming with light is the sea that sways gently,
Blue in the distance and softened by haze.
Long brooding headlands and far-away hillcrests
Set in perspective the sweep of the bays.

On comes the tide with a thousandfold whisper:
Waves gain momentum as shorewards they reach.
Breakers, advancing, receding, advancing,
Line with white crescents the smooth golden beach.

Water meets rock with a thud of defiance.
Droplets fly up, an explosion of spray.
Pebbles grind angrily, caught in the undertow;
Pouring through fissures, the surf runs away.

Masonry fallen from ramparts primeval,
Masses of limestone lie facing the sea.
Cliffs slope above them to heather and bracken:
Gorse blossoms gaily, but never a tree.

Aeons of time have perfected the landscape:
Little derives from the action of man.
This gives him meaning - to contemplate deeply,
Holding his vision as long as he can.

D A Hewitt

DARTMOOR

Out of the snug, smug village
over the cattle-grid onto the moor;
moor of myth and menace,
moor of lonely steadings and fierce wild freedom.

Ever-changing through the constant contours,
colours weave their kaleidoscope
among the gnarled and twisted trunks
of gorse and ancient trees.

Colours of earth, of bracken, muted; dun,
or burnished amber by the sun.
Subtly scented gorse - golden hued and fiecely prickled -
home to tunnel spiders with their early dewy webs.

Fir plantations hazy green and blue,
Alder catkins misty mauve above the jagged silver streams
with boulders smooth and cool -
perfect seats for secret dreams.

The moor's dark side is dark indeed.
Black the clouds that gather,
and the mist with all pervading speed
obliterates all points of reference.
This place - so beautiful,
when you can see
the boggy ground, the treacherous path,
the mud and overhanging branch -
is suddenly your enemy.

But, for me, a child of town,
adult of neat village and tame countryside,
the moors provide my momentary yearning for release.

M K L McConnell

IN THE GARDEN

Peacefulness in the morning,
as a new day is dawning.
The birds are calling from their nest,
that's what I like best, and all the rest.
When the sun is just aglow,
making everything grow.
As it comes up over the hill, shining
on my plants on the windowsill.
Then a shower of rain beat down on my windowpane,
all is fine in our garden again,
as flowers bloom, vegetables too, shrubs, trees in breezes,
as the wind changes.
In our lovely garden.

Kit Bolton

HAMPSHIRE THE HEAVENLY COUNTY

Hampshire means our heritage great,
small hamlets hidden, with
tea-cosied cottages.
High hills and valleys deep,
purple heather and heathlands dry.

Highways and byways, hustle and bustle,
and motorists hurtling by.
Hay fields and harvesting, and
heavy horses heaving.
heavenly spires upwardly soaring.

Hidden woodlands and New Forest sanctuaries.
Henry Tudor's hunting grounds, his hovering hawks
and harnesses glinting.
Hazy skies with thermal spirals and overhead
gliders on high.

Heaving seas and harbours safe.
High craggy hills and holiday beaches.
Hounds and huntsman, hackers and hikers.
Hordes of tourists eagerly visiting, and
hidden places where sun-worshippers lie.

Historic towns, and quiet havens.
Country crafts, and industries modern.
Gift shops and tea shops, and
olde worlde taverns.
Harmony and peace in Hampshire.

D L Hall

THE MOTH

A gay lepidoptera I do be,
that's a moth to you and me.
With my flimsies at the woggle
and my chompers at the ready,
I've just come back from a tasty snack
on a big fat furry teddy.
Now off I must go to old Mrs Fawcett's
to chomp my way through her brand new carpets!

K Leonard

RAIN FOR THE GARDEN

My granddad is happy when it's raining
He says it makes his garden grow
Why he talks so much about his garden
I'll really never know

My grandma loves the sunshine
She likes to get a good suntan
Be careful now says grandad
While filling up his watering can.

But grandma only puts more cream on
Then turns herself about
And you be careful too dear
Just remember there's a drought.

But grandad takes no notice
And waters every plant so well
Then he smiles and calls over
Now isn't that a lovely smell?

They once went to the Algarve
It rained most of the time
But not on granddad's garden
In England it was fine.

Pauline Kavanagh

THE PALACE OF THE HERON

Between the rolling mists of morn
Shadows cross the dewy lawn
Silhouettes against a charcoal sky
Two laden mules and one is I

Like soldiers from the trenches tread
Through thicket barbed wire
Brambles thread
What sense or instinct leads us here?
The voice of shingle or froth of weir
(Or distant mallard soothed the ear)

By gaslight our hallowed forms were lit
Two hunters in their staunchness sit
Swarthed against October's chill
Senses keen and bodies still

Surrounded by the rhythmic flow
Dance reflecting moonlight glow
And below,
Yes, below
Amid the rushing swirls and hiss
We mine for silver jewels
Us mortals call fish.

Kevin King

THE LONGEST RUNNER BEAN

To join a class I did aspire
To win a prize was my desire
The biggest longest runner bean
This whole village had ever seen!

I dug the holes, each one - two seeds
And gave my plantlets every need
I watered morning, noon and night
And kept a watch for every blight!

122

Like Jack's beanstalk they reached up high
On and on, on towards the sky
In wind and rain and sunshine too
I camped out there in misty dew!

Each time I measured straight and tall
My heart grew proud at one and all
The full round pods, so soft and green
Were quite the best I'd ever seen!

The day dawned bright, no rain to see
I gently picked, each wrapped by me
I trotted quickly to the hall
Fell over bench and broke them all!

Louise C Evans

UNTITLED

Blackbirds darting, fishes gliding
       Garden blooming, snails a-sliding
Grass is damp, June the date,
       Sky is pearly, dinner's late!
My love is lost, the past is done
       The ripples on the pool are gone
Like the memory of things past
       So bright they are, but fade so fast
If I could but relive my days
       To find the error of my ways
I might become a better man
       But may, perhaps, be second ran.

P A Rusling

COLOURS OF SPRING

Purple, yellow, red and green,
Is it a rainbow, pray?
No, it is just my garden scene
This fresh spring day.

Purple pansies, bright-eyed faces
Laughing up at me,
And the crocus, stately chalice
Open to the bee.

Yellow daffodils all swaying
In the rough wind's game;
Primroses, shy and retiring,
Prim, just like their name.

Red, the earliest of tulips,
Heart a golden star;
And the peony shoots just showing,
Bright, bright red they are.

Green the leaves all shapes and sizes,
Just as beautiful;
Green the grass, and green the weeds,
All a perfect foil.

Purple, yellow, red and green,
A rainbow of my own,
From seed and soil, from sun and rain,
This heaven on earth has grown.

K Pateman

BEATING MIDDLE-AGE SPREAD

Sweatshirt, shorts, trainers on
Half-past-six, time's getting on.
Knock! Knock! Pat's arrived, time to jog for two or three miles.
Hi Pauline! Ready and fit?
I see you've got on your new kit.
What a sight - off we go,
I hope we don't see someone we know.
Up the hill, down the other side,
round by the school, soon be out of sight.
Oh no! He's cutting his grass,
he'll stop for an eyeful when we jog past.
Head down, hide your face,
funny how we suddenly increase our pace.
Country lanes, nice and quiet,
let's slow down, for half-a-mile.
nearly home, increase in pace,
legs are aching, bright red face,
Neighbours watching through curtains of lace.
Must keep going, gate in sight,
God we'll sleep like logs tonight.
We made it!

Pauline Willicombe

WAR GAMES

The drums then rolled
As the Confederates proceeded;
The Unions were all alone.
The Rebels fought no end,
For Dixieland their home.

The children would cry,
Is Daddy going to die?
Mom knew he feared the war
But for the children she would lie.

Early on that stormy day,
The soldier on the floor did lay.
Only the children did not know
Daddy died long ago!

Stop! How can this be so,
It is extremely sad, but only a show.
To spend so much time like this
As entertainment I know.
I think next time I'll give it a miss!

L Griffiths

BOOKWORM

Today I'll get away from rain
and lie on a tropical beach
maybe I'll fly to sunny Spain
it's all within my reach.

One day dining with the rich
then tomorrow with a Lord
having tea at the Ritz
so how could I be bored?

Felt hunger in the Gorbals
walked streets of old Glasgow
with women wrapped in shawls
in winters of long ago.

Walked and talked with Cockneys
without rising from my chair
I can go where I please
my book will take me there.

S Wheelans

48